novum 🐦 pocket

AF273171

Re Par

The Supreme Power of the Universe

novum 📖 pocket

© 2023 novum publishing

ISBN 978-3-903468-40-5
Cover photo:
Rashevskaya I Dreamstime.com
Cover design, layout & typesetting:
novum publishing

www.novum-publishing.co.uk

CONTENTS

PREFACE

My goal in writing this book is to open a window to the higher worlds and dimensions and to remind humanity of the lost paradise we have been away from for so long that we believe the heavens is the same world we are living in now. As the title of the book reflects, the focus is on a comprehensive and single force that controls the entire system of the universe with all dimensions and creatures within it. This infinite power unconsciously conjures up the phrase **the supreme power of the universe** in my mind, and that is why I decided to choose this phrase as the title of my book. I recently watched the TV series *Ancient Aliens*, and it gave me some interesting ideas. Contrary to traditional beliefs, the theorists of this TV series have tried to prove the presence of some invisible beings with superior technologies and a brain capacity much larger than that of humans in the universe. Interdimensional beings have been visiting Earth for millions of years and are believed to have spread the first seeds of life on Earth. Therefore, it can be said that they are the creator gods of human beings and of all kinds of animal and plant species on Earth. However, there is undoubtedly no existence without a creator, and since only one absolute power can be the creator of the entire universe with all intelligent and non-intelligent beings in it, including interdimensional beings, humans, animals and plants, then the idea of extraterrestrial beings as the creator gods of humans in no way jeopardizes the existence of the absolute lord of all dimensions of the universe, but it can also be some strong evidence of the existence of a powerful creator god by providing some evidence of antiquity.

If we consider the interdimensional beings known as the Anunnaki in the Mesopotamian civilization (the oldest known human civilization after the great flood) as the creators of mankind, the Supreme Power of the Universe should also be considered the sole creator god of the interdimensional beings. So, there is indeed an absolute creator god in all dimensions of the Universe who is indirectly the prime creator of humanity and rules all worlds of existence. In order to reach the Lord (S.P.U.), it is not necessary to seek her/him physically in the worlds of existence. God is not a finite physical body residing in a specific place; rather, God is a kind of infinite energy that encompasses all worlds of existence. In fact, God is the whole dimension of existence. Stars, planets, celestial bodies, extraterrestrial beings, humans, animals, plants, and objects are all part of this absolute and unlimited wisdom. In other words, God (S.P.U.) is the whole dimension of existence with all its affiliations; the essence capable of creating itself from nothing and constantly presents in all dimensions of existence, overseeing all affairs of the worlds and all creatures inhabiting them. God is sun, Earth, sky, mountain, tree, plain, desert, rain, snow, day, night, stars, planets, and celestial meteors. God is in us. God is everything.

Fourteen billion years ago, the only god of all dimensions suddenly created the physical world before our eyes with a big explosion (the Big Bang). After the Big Bang, two types of energy were released in the universe – positive and negative energies. Positive energy is the fuel and source of positive and constructive actions in the universe. However, negative energy is the driving force of evil actions and destructive events in the universe. Storms, earthquakes, volcanic eruptions, tornadoes, etc. – all these disasters do not happen by themselves, but they all happen due to the presence of negative energy in the environment. Positive and negative energies are the spirit, wisdom, and consciousness of the universe and, according to the Yin & Yang theory, they complement each other like night and day and black and white, so one has no meaning without the other. The combination of these two forces creates an infinite power in the name of the Supreme Power of the Universe, which is present in all dimensions and worlds of existence at every moment and supervises all human behaviour and affairs. It is not only humans who have intelligence, but all animals, plants, and even objects have a sense of wisdom. The wisdom of a tree is to be a tree. The wisdom of a mountain is to be a mountain. And the wisdom of a stone is to be like a piece of stone. In other words, nothing in this world is unconscious.

Everything around us has its own reason and logic. When the Anunnaki gods first created the human body hundreds of thousands of years ago, they breathed into it the divine and positive energy of the universe to give it life – the same divine spiritual energy that exists in all extraterrestrial and interdimensional beings. In the path of spiritual and mental evolution, man commits a series of negative actions under the influence of negative energy around him. These sins leave black spots on the spirit of a person. When the volume of these black spots increases, the speed of spiritual evolution and correct mental development of a person decreases. However, with the physical death of a person, those people who have not been able to achieve sufficient spiritual development and proper mental evolution, and have black spots in their spirits, cannot enter the heavens directly. This group of people, which includes a large part of humans, are sent to another world, called purgatory, for reform and training. In purgatory, people are treated and trained for long periods, depending on the number of sins they had committed in their previous lives. Only human beings whose spirits are free from any blackness and filth are taken directly to the Garden of Paradise by the divine spirits and Anunnaki angels after physical death, while most human spirits are reincarnated in new bodies on Planet Earth after being treated and trained in purgatory to be tested once again in a different situation. In this way, extraterrestrial gods place people in new situations based on their past life performance and spiritual quality, thereby retesting their performance and administering justice.

Every extraterrestrial being that appeared in prehistoric times and pretended to be a god, exploiting the ignorance of primitive people and substituting science and technology for miracles, was actually an idol or false god. Merely creating a creature through scientific methods cannot confer god status on anyone, since these extraterrestrial beings themselves are the creation of another almighty god. Therefore, these interdimensional beings can only be viewed as intermediary and subsidiary gods between the Absolute Lord of the Universe (SPU) and humanity. Unfortunately, like the common people, the prophets also made the same mistake. Throughout history, several ascetics gained the ability to spiritually communicate with other dimensions due to austerity, while this work came with access to all the sciences of existence known as Akashic Records. As a result of long austerity and meditation, these people gained such strength of mind and will that they were able to access the Vril energy, which is the main energy of the universe.

With their physical encounters with extraterrestrial beings, prophets and saints mistook them for gods or supernatural beings, which they called angels.

However, aliens used the same method to make themselves appear as gods and impose their will on humans after seeing humans' reactions to their technologies and their seductive effect on them. After observing those, the aliens used the same method to make themselves appear as gods so that they could impose their will on humans.

These extraterrestrial beings were the creation of another almighty god. The truth is not easy to obtain, and one must find it to find it, although 100% truth can never be reached, and it is better to accept a set of dubious theories that have yet to be proven than to live in ignorance and darkness. Considering the various theories that discuss the philosophy of creation, those that help us to know God better commit fewer sins in our lives.

AUTHOR'S NOTE

I remember one warm afternoon about 17 years ago when I was in a light sleep, I could feel the shadow of a being or something else above my head. It was almost like smoke, but after I opened my eyes, it suddenly evaporated. About 15 years later, one night, I dreamed that I was following a UFO with my finger. When this UFO stopped in mid-air at the end of the street, I quickly reached under it. At that moment, some strange creatures, like the Roswell aliens, opened the door of the UFO and looked at me. It was at that moment that I suddenly woke up. I've always felt that I was made for a special mission, something beyond the daily chores of marriage, procreation and ...

THE CREATION

About 13.7 billion years ago, by the will of the Supreme Power of the Universe, an infinitesimally small proton particle of infinitely high density suddenly appeared out of nowhere. When this particle exploded a little later, an infinite amount of energy was released in a few seconds, and as this energy level gradually cooled, stars, black holes, galaxies, and planets began to form. About 4.5 billion years have passed since Planet Earth existed. In the beginning, the Earth lacked water, oxygen, and life. Due to the impacts of meteorites on the Earth's surface, water gradually came into being on Planet Earth. During this time, the Earth's temperature was so high due to the many volcanic activities and meteorite impacts.

After the volcanic activities and meteorite impacts on the Earth's surface subsided, cyanobacteria, which are naturally trapped in meteorites as life seeds in space, reached Earth about 3.7 billion years ago. Since these cyanobacteria live in the ice layers of meteorites, which are themselves surrounded by dust particles, and since the dust particles isolate radioactivity in space, these cyanobacteria can live on in the meteorites. These cyanobacteria, or the same blue-green algae that existed in the stromatolite rocks, gradually began to photosynthesize oxygen. In this process, which lasted millions of years, unicellular and multicellular plants and animals emerged. The evolutionary process of life on Earth continued until finally, about 70 million years ago, in the age of the dinosaurs and at the end of the Cretaceous Period, the first intelligent extraterrestrial beings set foot on Planet Earth. The ancient extraterrestrials have inhabited the Earth for 70 million years and, in fact, the extraterrestrials are the true creators of mankind.

In the beginning, there lived other groups of beings called elves, created by the same gods of Mesopotamia, the Anunnaki. These horned humanoids had long, pointed ears like a donkey, two hooves, and a tail. They lived on Planet Earth for millions of years and reached the highest level of technology with the help of the Anunnaki. But, during their lives on Earth, they were always busy with evil, killing, and plundering. As a result, the Anunnaki gods decided to replace them on the planet with a new species. So, the elves were banished to the underworld, hell.

After the Anunnaki sent the elves from Planet Earth to the underworld about 6 million years ago, they created species of great apes, including Habilis, Erectus, Rudolfensis, Heidelbergensis, Floresiensis, Neanderthalensis, Naledi, Luzonensis, and Homo sapiens by making genetic changes in monkeys.

The history of the Sumerian civilization goes back to about 4,500 years B.C., which is considered the oldest among other human civilizations, such as Egyptians, Mayans, Greeks, Persians, Indians, Chinese, etc. In southern Mesopotamia lies the city of Ur, which dates back to 3,800 B.C. Ur is the birthplace of the Prophet Abraham. Twelve kilometres south of Ur is a city called Eridu, which dates back to 5,400 B.C. Eridu is considered the first capital of the Sumerian civilization.

In 1849, famous English archaeologist Austen Henry Layard managed to discover the palace of Sennacherib buried underground near the citadel walls of Nineveh. Three years later, his assistant managed to discover another palace right in front of the Palace of Sennacherib, which belonged to Sennacherib's grandson, Ashurbanipal. In both palaces, there were libraries containing tens of thousands of clay tablets written in cuneiform. Seven of these clay tablets, known as the Enūma Eliš, tell the story of the creation of man by supernatural beings called the Anunnaki.

According to these clay tablets, the Anunnaki came back to Earth, through the Nibiru Stargate 450,000 years ago, to extract gold from the Abzu mines. The remains of approximately 200,000-year-old gold mining sites have recently been found in South Africa, consistent with Sumerian descriptions of the Abzu mines and Anunnaki gold-mining activities in prehistoric times. In fact, the massive stone circle complexes are remnants of Tesla-like technology used to generate electricity and tunnels dug directly into the ground.

Every 3,600 years, the Nibiru stargate, which has an elliptical orbit, reaches its closest distance to Earth. Nibiru is the ninth star (stargate) in the solar system after Neptune. The temperature of the Anunnaki's planet, which is in a higher dimension than Planet Earth, was so hot due to volcanic activities, making it difficult to breathe and causing a large gap in that planet's ozone layer. This situation caused a rebellion among the people of this planet so Alalu, one of the Anunnaki's princes, assassinated their king (the God). After the Anunnaki's king was killed, Alalu and Anu (nephew of the murdered king and the legal heir) fought in a battle in which Anu defeated Alalu (Satan) and successfully attained the position of kingship (the position of God).

After losing the battle, Alalu went to Planet Earth to recover his lost credit and save their planet. Finally, after a long journey, he was able to reach Planet Earth. Immediately after discovering gold in the mines of Abzu, Alalu contacted the Anunnaki and told them everything.

Eventually, a group of Anunnaki men (the Angels), under the command of Aa, boarded their ships to Planet Earth by order of King Anu (the new God). It was a long and arduous journey. At first, many of them got sick, the days and nights of the Earth were so short for them. After seven days and nights of uninterrupted work, they were finally able to build the city of Eridu. Then, they quickly began mining gold in the mines of Abzu. Initially, gold extraction from the mines went well, and the transit of gold powder to the Anunnaki's planet to restore its atmosphere was successful, but the good days didn't last long for Aa.

Eventually, Anlil (King Anu's son by an official marriage) came to Planet Earth to take over the commanding position of the planet, and there was a heated debate between Anlil and Aa (King Anu's eldest son by an unofficial marriage) on who should be the commander.

Meanwhile, Alalu also claimed to rule until King Anu himself intervened to resolve the crisis and personally set foot on Planet Earth. After King Anu came to Planet Earth, he summoned Alalu to a naked fight, according to the customs. They fought each other, and King Anu won the battle again. Instead of giving the order to kill Alalu, King Anu banished him to the planet Mars to be a lesson for others. The human face imprinted on the surface of Mars is actually the tomb of Alalu. After Anlil become the ruler of the Earth, he was called Enki. The Anunnaki decided to build a stargate on the planet Mars to facilitate the transportation of gold from Earth, so they no longer had to travel the long journey to Nibiru. Marduk, Anki's eldest son took responsibility for this.

Gold extraction from the Abzu mines continued until the Anunnaki decided to create a new being to work in the mines. By order of Anu (the Lord) Ninmah, Anki's half-sister and her son, Ningishzida, were entrusted with this work. Many efforts were made to create this new creature. They tried to genetically modify Neanderthal sperm and then place it in the uterus of a female monkey, but the result was unsatisfactory. After many but unsuccessful attempts, the Anunnaki finally decided, as a last resort, to collect the sperm of a Neanderthal. Then, they added the FAXP2 gene (the language gene) to its DNA, which is the same exact gene that crosses the line between human and animal, and placed it in the womb of an Anunnaki woman and created this new creature. For this, Anki's half-sister Ninmah was chosen by Anu (the God). Eventually, the new being was born, and he was named Adamu. After the birth of Adamu, the Anunnaki created a female named Eve to mate with him and spread the Homo sapien race on Earth. So, Adamu and Eve had sex with each other and created the Homo sapien generation, i.e., the toolmakers and intelligent people who could talk on the planet.

At that time, the temperature of the Earth was much colder than today, and, at its hottest point, the temperature reached a maximum of 9 degrees Celsius (48 degrees Fahrenheit).

The political system of the Anunnaki was structured in the form of a hierarchy, meaning the king who was residing on the planet of the Anunnaki in the upper dimension was at the head of all affairs. And, in the lower ranks, there were princes and princesses who were occasionally chosen as the commanders of those planets, which were under the control of the Anunnaki. But the extraterrestrial Anunnaki, who ruled Earth, still held lower positions than the princes and princesses, who were on the planet of the Anunnaki.

Since Planet Earth was in a lower position (material dimension) compared to the Anunnaki's planet, the Anunnaki used Planet Earth as a place of banishment for the fallen Anunnaki (fallen angels). In fact, the purpose of creating humans on Planet Earth was not just to create a workforce or a sex tool, but to create bodies for the sinful souls of the Anunnaki. These sinful souls were forced to endure all the pains and hardships of living in a human body for at least one Earthly life. Only after all their sins were washed away could they then regain their eternal and luminous nature. But we humans are all extraterrestrials in origin, and we still hope for God's mercy and forgiveness in hopes of regaining our angelic nature and returning to our original home, which is somewhere in a higher dimension. Moreover, there is another world lower than our Earthly world, which is called Hell. Evil spirits, demons, elves, and evil people live there.

The Anunnaki Commanders, who ruled Planet Earth, were a group of Anunnaki angels, each with a specific responsibility. The highest of them was in charge of the affairs of the rest; on the Mesopotamian clay tablets, he is called Enlil or Enki. Another one was the angel of death, Yahman Azrael. The Anunnaki and the human hybrids have ruled over mankind since the creation of mankind. The clay tablet of Enūma Eliš, discovered in fragments in Ashurbanipal's ruined library at Nineveh by English archaeologist Austen Henry Layard in 1849, provides evidence for this claim. This tablet contains the list of kings who ruled the land of Mesopotamia over hundreds of generations. It is interesting that, on this list, there are names of kings who lived for a long time, like 36,000 years, 43,000 years, 21,000 years and so on.

Further evidence for this claim is the discovery of the remains of Queen Puabi in the Ur Royal Cemetery. Her skull is unusually elongated like the skulls of the Anunnaki gods seen in Sumerian carvings. Queen Puabi lived around 2,600 B.C. in Mesopotamia and is believed to have been the second wife of the Sumerian king Meskalamdug.

The half-god, half-man kings and queens of ancient times took pride in their different appearances because it gave them a sense of racial superiority towards ordinary people. For this reason, they wanted their images to be carved on the walls of their palaces and tombs with a precise appearance, that is, with elongated skulls. For example, in ancient Egypt, Akhenaten insisted that his image be engraved on the walls of his palace and tomb exactly as it was. In these images, one can see Akhenaten's protruding abdomen, chicken like legs, and his long and elongated skull, showing his half-human and half-divine nature. Indeed, all kings and prominent historical figures, who had an elongated skull, had a semi-divine nature, including Noah, Methuselah (Noah's father).

In the border region between Lebanon and Syria, there is a mountain called Mount Hermon that is believed to be the place where hundreds of thousands of years ago a group of 200 angels landed. The duty of these angels was monitoring human actions on Earth. In the beginning, these angels had to take an oath of loyalty to the Lord (Anu) so that under no circumstances engage in sexual relations with any Earthly woman. This oath was taken because the angels who had come from the higher dimension (the Anunnaki's planet or Heaven) were equipped with some sort of technological capability that enabled them to change from the spiritual phase to the physical phase. But when they entered the physical phase, their sexual desires came alive in them; hence, they were always in danger of having sex with the Earthly women. These angels are also called the guardians. Unfortunately, these angels could not keep their oath. Gradually, the angels began having sex with the Earthly women. The result of these sexual relations were gigantic creatures called the Nephilim. But this disrupted the process of human evolution, which the aliens had started 70 million years ago.

As a result of this disobedience, God's wrath rose and led to a celestial battle between the Anunnaki extraterrestrials living in the upper dimension and the fallen extraterrestrials. In this battle, the Anunnaki angels defeated the fallen angels. Among the names that can be given to these fallen angels are Apollo, Hera, Poseidon, Horus, Neptune, Lucifer, and Prometheus.

DHUL-QARNAIN

Thousands of years ago, a very powerful person lived on Earth. Thanks to the power that God gave him, he could travel from east to west, north to south, and to any part of the world in a matter of seconds. His goal was to introduce God and the system of creation to mankind. If we have security today, one of the reasons is the service that Dhul-Qarnain proposed to mankind thousands of years ago. But the enemies of mankind, i.e., elves and demons, still live, waiting for the day they can attack us again.

Dhul-Qarnain was famous for his travels as he is said to have been a time traveller. The word Dhul-Qarnain means time traveller. It means someone who can travel between the present and the past. Dhul-Qarnain had three famous voyages, one of which is more important than the other two voyages. On his first voyage, Dhul-Qarnain went to a place where the sun sets. There, he saw the sun going down in a black hole that he had probably gone near. On his second trip, he went to a planet where the sun never sets, and the people there had no cover from the sun and were constantly exposed to radioactive radiation.

Finally, for his last journey, which is more important than the rest, he went to a place in the middle of the mountains, and there he met a group of people who, upon seeing his strong body, asked him to protect them against the harassment of some evil creatures called Gog and Magog. Indeed, Gog and Magog were the evil djinns who could come to Earth from the underworld through, creating a stargate that appeared between two mountains.

Dhul-Qarnain, who was half-alien and half-human, knew the causes of all these terrible incidents with his great knowledge and knew effective solutions to solve these crises. He had received all his knowledge from his alien gods. After hearing their problem, Dhul-Qarnain told them to gather as much iron as possible and put it between the two mountains from which the elves appeared. Then Dhul-Qarnain asked them to pour molten copper onto the pieces of iron. When the copper was cold enough, Dhul-Qarnain cast a spell on that wall so that Gog and Magog could no longer use that stargate to enter Earth. This is one of the signs of the Apocalypse because, just before the Apocalypse, this spell will be reversed, and Gog and Magog will attack humanity from this stargate. But when will the Apocalypse really take place? According to Leonardo da Vinci, the Apocalypse will take place on March 21, 4006. He believed that on that very day, the world will be destroyed by a great flood akin to Noah's flood.

JOURNEY OF THE SPIRIT

In general, the Universe consists of two different dimensions:

1. The visible and physical matrix in which Planet Earth and hell (the Underworld) reside, and
2. The matrix wherein purgatory (where the soul goes after the death of a human or animal) and paradise reside.

The underworld (Hell) is where demons and djinns live, and heaven is the place of eternal spirits, the world of salvation, and planet of the gods. The spirits of humans and animals are sent to purgatory to get processed for a certain period after death. How long a spirit must remain in purgatory depends on its actions and behaviours in the former life. If the spirit has experienced a righteous life before death, it is sent immediately to the higher dimension – paradise. Paradise itself has thirteen different levels.

But, if this spirit belongs to a criminal, it will only go to hell. However, if the spirit has not fully lived out its previous life on Earth, for example, and died by suicide or was aborted at birth, it cannot enter paradise. Spirits who have committed suicide in their previous lives go straight to hell, and the spirits of those who were aborted at birth in their previous lives must wait in purgatory until some suitable bodies are found for their new lives on Earth. Usually, people who were aborted at birth find their new bodies in the same families as their previous ones. In this case, it is possible that the incarnation would take place two or 20 years later.

However, the spirits of those who were martyred in war in defence of a sacred value will ascend straight to heaven. In this state, the spirit, which has an immortal and indestructible nature, has a luminous body and possesses powers that allow it to travel between different dimensions and interstellar spaces. Although, the spirits of those who have committed crimes on the battlefield go straight to hell. The rest are reborn on Earth in new bodies. In this case, it is said that, although these people have committed murder while serving in the military, because of their other good qualities, God has given them the opportunity to come back to Earth to make up for the sins of their past lives. Also, for people who have died in car accidents, plane crashes, shipwrecks, train derailments, fires, etc., or during childbirth, their spirits are reincarnated in new human bodies on Earth to resume their new lives and be tested again. It is better to endure the hardships of life to the end rather than to commit suicide because man may not even find a chance to be resurrected on Earth and instead is sent straight to hell.

For both spirit and body, commuting between different dimensions, like paradise, hell, purgatory, etc., is possible only through the stargates. Stargates exist both naturally and unnaturally in the universe. For example, Nibiru is a natural stargate that approaches Earth once every 3,600 years. Today, we can find the remains of some of the man-made stargates at the ancient sites. Some of these stargates are in the form of keyholes carved into large blocks of stones. They can also be found in special caves. For example, a stargate is believed to be in the Hal-Saflieni Hypogeum Cave, located in Paola, Malta.

The world we live in is surrounded by 12 zodiac signs. In other words, the 12 zodiac constellations form the boundary between our dimension (the physical and visible world: Earth and Hell) and the spiritual dimension (Paradise and Purgatory). The 12 zodiac signs are Aries, Taurus, Gemini, Cancer, Leo, Virgo, Libra, Scorpio, Sagittarius, Capricorn, Aquarius, and Pisces. Between the constellations Virgo and Libra is a Stargate that shines like a very bright star in the sky. In the zodiac circle, all the stargates are interconnected and lead to a main stargate, which is located between the constellations Virgo and Libra. This stargate is called the Mother Stargate. Basically, all the minor stargates in the zodiac circle, including the Sirius stargate, the Orion stargate, and the Pleiades stargate, lead to this mother stargate. In fact, that is the exit gate from our physical dimension to other dimensions, such as heaven and purgatory. Also, the souls of the dead travel through the same stargate into the spiritual dimension. It is also possible to make artificial and small stargates, but they are not strong or large enough to transport people from one dimension to another.

Recently, scientists from the European Organization for Nuclear Research (CERN) in Switzerland have managed to use the Large Hadron Collider (LHC) to detect the massive particles, like Higgs boson, the quarks and gluons, through accelerating protons at speeds close to the speed of light and colliding them against each other. According to string theory, the smallest particles in the universe are some sort of vibrating threads, which are even smaller than the Higgs boson particles.

In general, the universe consists of two different dimensions: the spiritual and the physical. The spiritual matrix, like a blanket, covers the visible matrix. In fact, these two totally different dimensions of the universe have their own unique rules. If, in the physical dimension, for example, $3 \times 3 = 9$, it doesn't mean that it would be the same in the spiritual dimension. The spiritual dimension includes two worlds: heaven and purgatory. The physical dimension, which is where we are currently living, contains Earth and hell. Hell is in the smallest layers of the universe; that's why it is called the underworld. Our physical and visible world that we are currently living in is itself surrounded by a higher world called purgatory. Purgatory is like a hospital where the extraterrestrial angels try to cleanse the human spirit from any ugliness and blackness and prepare it for life again on Earth. The Garden of Heaven, which is the abode of gods and angels, is also located in the same dimension. Only pure and holy spirits can enter heaven. There, the pure spirits live forever in peace and harmony in a world free from pain and suffering. But nothing is truly eternal, and that is a principle in the universe. The only thing that destroys this spiritual immortality and that can cause the fall of the angels and drive them out of heaven is disobedience to God's commandments and breaking the laws of heaven.

However, just as people on Earth have their own positions, the holy spirits in heaven have different ranks. God is at the highest level, followed by angels and then other holy spirits. But the most important technological ability that pure spirits have in heaven is the ability to transition from the spiritual level to the physical level. In other words, these pure spirits are capable of assuming a physical body. But when they assume a material form, they are again exposed to desires and pain. There is also the risk that, due to committing sins, they would lose their heavenly positions and fall into the lower dimension for a long period of time. Perhaps this was the reason for the disobedience and the fall of the guardian angels. Prometheus, who was once one of the closest and most beautiful angels of God and was called Lucifer, which means something like the Bringer of the Knowledge for mankind, disregarded God's commandment by giving science and technology to primitive peoples who did not yet have the mental capacity to handle that amount of knowledge. In this way, he disturbed the order and balance of creation.

As punishment, God threw him out of heaven and imprisoned his spirit in an ordinary human body. As Prometheus was banished to Planet Earth, he lost all his extraterrestrial abilities as well. In general, all human beings were once angels and lived as angels in eternal heaven, but because they committed sins and disobeyed God, they were transferred to the lower worlds, and, because of this transition, they lost many of their former abilities. But that wasn't the whole story. Even after that, many fallen angels continued on their wrong path and committed innumerable sins on Earth for the second time. This time, however, they descended into a lower world, which was hell. But, like heaven and Earth, hell has innumerable ranks and stages; the more sins a person commits, the lower his/her status.

In Dante's *Divine Comedy*, hell has nine layers and each layer is specific to a particular sin. Fallen humans are classified and tortured in each of these layers based on the quality and quantity of their sins.

- The first layer is Limbo.
- The second layer is Lust.
- The third layer is Gluttony.
- The fourth layer is Stinginess;
- The fifth layer is Anger and Sloth.
- The sixth layer is Heresy.
- The seventh layer is Violence.
- The eighth layer is Fraud.
- And the last and ninth layer is Treason.

The position of man and angels, whether good or evil, constantly alternates between the layers of heaven, hell, and Earth. The comfort and well-being of angels and good men, and the pain and suffering of sinful men and fallen angels, are by no means eternal. Youth, beauty, health, old age, ugliness, sickness, happiness, joy, sorrow, wealth, fame, poverty, scandal, insecurity, security and comfort are not eternal, but they change like the seasons of the year.

> **Every night and every morning,**
> **Some to misery are born.**
> **Every morning and every night,**
> **Some are born to Sweet Delight,**
> **Some are born to Sweet Delight,**
> **Some are born to Endless Night.**
> *William Blake*

ALIEN DEMONS

But who are the devils? Where are they coming from? What is their goal?

Humans have never been alone on Earth and have always been threatened by extraterrestrial beings. Aliens come to us secretly without us noticing their presence. Basically, every extraterrestrial being, other than the Anunnaki gods and angels, who are the creators of us humans, is called Satan. Indeed, these evil extraterrestrial beings come to Planet Earth from distant planets in higher dimensions with the highly developed technologies at their disposal, and then they seduce humans. However, not all of these extraterrestrial beings have hostile targets. Some of them do research only on humans. But some others who are in competition with the Anunnaki gods have no other aim than the destruction of humanity and possession of Planet Earth. These evil extraterrestrials or demons come from the higher dimension that has surrounded our world. They come to Earth and, like all extraterrestrial beings, have supernatural capabilities and are equipped with very advanced technologies that cannot even be imagined. One of these technologies is the ability to transition from the spiritual phase to the physical phase and vice versa.

Throughout history, the extraterrestrial demons have always been travelling to Earth in their spaceships. These creatures occasionally kidnap humans and take them to their spaceships and perform certain experiments on them. The purpose of these human abductions is to prepare an army of human and alien hybrids. To do this, they do not act directly, but use alien-robot hybrids. These alien-robot hybrids are known as grey aliens. Although these intelligent alien robots are highly advanced and can do things that even the smartest of humans are unable to do, unlike their alien creators, they are unable to go from the physical state to the spiritual state. They also need a spaceship to travel in space. They look like insects or mole crickets. They are dark blue, green, and grey in colour. Usually, a kind of oil oozes out of them, and they always leave behind a fluorescent effect. In fact, these alien intelligent robots have been created by alien demons for use in our physical world.

In 1947, a UFO crashed in the town of Roswell, New Mexico, in the United States. Shortly thereafter, the bodies of several strange grey creatures were found by local authorities in the remains of the crashed UFO. Apparently, the release of radioactivity in space caused this UFO to crash. Unfortunately, all the strange creatures were found dead, except one. When the creature was taken to a military hospital for treatment, the alien creature implanted some information into its head via telepathy, according to a nurse who was present in the operating room at the time. According to this alien creature, we humans have been created by another group of extraterrestrial beings and, in fact, belong to another dimension and world. However, it is very difficult for us to leave this world and return to our original world, even spiritually.

After the 1947 UFO crash in Roswell, American experts were able to reverse engineer a similar UFO. Using some sort of anti-gravity technology, these UFOs can reach speeds close to the speed of light. As a result, tracking these UFOs with even the most advanced radars is very difficult. Today, some of the armies of the world, including the United States, are equipped with these ultrasonic UFOs, but to prevent terrorists from accessing them, they have kept the technology a secret until today. Among the other technologies that American scientists have achieved through the use of reverse engineering is a type of technology with which one can disable or bring under control all electronic systems of vehicles, such as aeroplanes, fighter jets, ships, etc. With this technology, one can force the planes that fly in the sky to land on the ground. This type of technology is also used in artificial UFOs.

The alien demons have always been actively in competition with our alien gods throughout history. They regularly kidnap humans and carry them into their ships and conduct medical experiments on them. For example, less than 15% of the world population has an RH negative blood type. The fact is that mankind has had this gene for less than 30,000 years, and it did not exist before that time. This gene is particularly abundant in the people of the Basque Country in Spain and France. People with this blood type can only have children or, if necessary, receive blood from their blood relatives. No one knows how this blood type suddenly entered human DNA, but it is definitely due to a genetic mutation, which is attributed to happening thousands of years ago.

Also, recently, green and hazel eye colours have been observed in humans, while only 3% of the world's population have green eyes. Normally, alien demons work on the 97% of our unused DNA that is still unknown to us. But their main goal is to create a group of hybrid humans of their own race, a sort of 'watchful soldier', always ready to carry out his/her mission when he/she receives a signal from them. According to the Apostle of Revelation, **'When the sinners are organized, and the comet appears, the Roman Empire will rise, and you and I will die here. He will rise from the raging sea. He will raise an army from all shores. This is the moment when he launches a terrible attack.'**

> 'Here is wisdom. Whoever has wisdom
> should count the number of the beast,
> for it is the number of a man,
> and his number is 666.'
> *Book of Revelation 13:18*

One of the most interesting cases of human abduction by extraterrestrials is the case of Jim Sparks. In 1988, he was abducted by a group of extraterrestrials from his home in the U.S. According to his own statements, while he was sleeping, he felt himself being pulled upward. He could see the roof of his house and the trees from above. He also remembered moving away from Planet Earth. He remembered several nesting corridors. He also described a great hall full of specimens of animals, plants, humans, and some kinds of strange creatures Jim had never seen before. The samples were semi-conscious and kept in laboratory jars. Jim recalled the aliens trying to teach him their own language and recalled drawing a series of parallel lines on a monitor. He also remembered a large monitor through which he could see the entire history of mankind from the modern era, the Roman Empire,

Ancient Egypt, the glory days of the Mesopotamia civilization to the Neanderthal era and even the era of the dinosaurs.

Many people abducted by aliens return after being paralyzed, unable to move, and having lost their memory and sense of time. Some of these abductees had implants placed in their bodies by aliens. However, not all abductions were performed by alien demons; some of them were actually performed by Anunnaki gods who have different names in different cultures, like Shiva, Brahma, Vishnu, Ganesha, Mithras, Anu, Aten, Enki, Kukulkan, Viracocha, etc. In other words, the same gods who created mankind. There is a sacred and humanitarian purpose behind all these kidnappings. One of the most famous ancient kidnappings is the story of the kidnapping of Priya Pisnokar, the architect of the palace at Angkor Wat, who is believed to have been a demigod. Apparently, Priya Pisnokar had undergone intensive architectural training during his alien abduction. Apparently, after Priya Pisnokar was brought back to Planet Earth by extraterrestrials, he began building Angkor Wat by order of the Khmer King Suryavarman II. Angkor Wat is located in Cambodia and covers an area of 162.6 hectares (about 402 acres). It is the largest religious building in the world built to worship Lord Vishnu.

COMMUNICATION WITH EXTRATERRESTRIALS

Before history and since primitive man knew his soul, he fought against the forces that wanted to enslave him. From the very beginning, he had perceived the opposing forces of nature: the evil eyes of the tiger, the terrifying rumble of thunder, the howling of the wind in the darkness that had gripped the human soul. Fear created superstition and rendered logic ineffective. He created tyrannical gods whose existence ruled human unity. Violence arose, and the human spirit was under the heel of the conqueror. But in the depths of the human heart, the fire of the urge for freedom still burned, and whenever these sparks were kindled in a man's soul, whether he was a priest or a soldier, a patriotic artist, a lover, or a politician, his deeds changed the course of human destiny and his name has remained in history forever.

There are many ways to communicate with extraterrestrials, whether Anunnaki gods or extraterrestrial demons. Jesus Christ, who is the Holy Spirit of God, himself, said, 'If two or three people are gathered in my name, I will be among them.' Normally, summoning spirits is done by sound. For example, the participants in the Mass allow the spirit of Jesus Christ to dissolve in them through singing in a group. In fact, with their bodies, they create a suitable platform to receive the great energy of the Spirit of Jesus Christ.

Latin American shamans also make a type of herbal medicine called Ayahuasca by combining two types of plants. By drinking this herbal decoction and dancing around the fire, they enter a trance state, which lets them observe some sort of visual illusions. In this state, their spirit rises to a higher dimension so that they can communicate with the spirits of extraterrestrial beings. The indigenous people of the Kalahari region in Africa have a similar ritual. By burning a certain type of plant in fire and dancing around it, they enter a trance state that lasts well into the night. In this state, they can even put their faces into the fire without hurting themselves or putting the hot coals in their mouths.

In fact, shamans and exorcists can use sound frequencies and the hypnotic power of certain ancient medicines to open specific stargates and channels through which they can communicate with extraterrestrials living in the higher worlds. Also, Indian ascetics, by eating dry bread, performing yoga movements naked and concentrating on a certain point, consuming marijuana and other ecstatic herbal drugs, bathing in the cold mountain air, standing on one leg for several days, dancing in groups and worshipping by the fire, after many years of austerity, they finally manage to burn off the karma within themselves, and go through the fourth stage of spiritual progression of the Hindu religion. When Hindu ascetics attain this level of willpower, they are able to do extraordinary things, such as sticking skewers into their bodies without feeling pain or losing a drop of blood; stopping a moving train by just looking at it, walking barefoot on fire and acquiring the knowledge of sciences, especially medicine; breaking a pane of glass by looking at it; summoning the spirits of extraterrestrial demons; and predicting future events. Therefore, in order to achieve spiritual excellence and strengthen their will, mystics, shamans, exorcists, and ascetics in all parts of the world basically rely on two methods:

1. Abstinence
2. Use of hypnotics.

This is exactly how they can connect to the higher worlds and summon the spirits of extraterrestrial beings.

NOAH'S FLOOD

Between 1946 and 1956, archaeologists discovered 800 papyrus scrolls in 11 caves near the ancient region of Qumran in Palestine, 16 kilometres (almost 10 miles) east of Jerusalem. These scrolls are known as the Dead Sea Scrolls and are housed along with the Book of Enoch in museums in Jerusalem, Israel and preserved in Jordan. These papyrus scrolls contain valuable information about the antediluvian era, the journey of Enoch, Noah's grand-father's father, and his encounter with God while de-scribing God's face as shining molten iron, as well as the Nephilim and the fall of 200 angels on Mount Hermon.

Hundreds of thousands of years ago, the Anunnaki gods created the toolmaker-vocal race of Homo sapiens by adding the FOXP2 gene to the DNA of another group of humanoid apes living in Africa, hoping that this new intelligent being would gradually progress through the various stages of evolution and attain a stage of intel-lectual maturity and technology suitable for the puni-tive purposes of extraterrestrial gods. The Anunnaki gods never intended to create man to be able to attain the same level of technology as the gods themselves who live in the upper worlds. Moreover, humans were never destined to achieve 100% evolution, so 97% of human DNA, still unknown to DNA experts, is useless, mean-ing we can only use 3% of our own DNA. The Anunnaki gods needed a semi-intelligent being of flesh and blood fit to live in a visible world so that it could hold the souls of the sinful angels who were banished to the physical dimension from the higher dimension. But extraterrestrial demons have always fought the Anunnaki gods for supremacy on Planet Earth.

As the extraterrestrial demons always wanted to rule their own generation on Earth, they created a new generation of giant humans, called the Nephilim, by engaging in sexual relations with Homo sapiens. These Nephilim giants, which were half-human and half-devil and sometimes reached a height of 30 metres (98.5 feet), were so evil and constantly killed and robbed ordinary people on Earth, who were much smaller than them. The Ād tribe, who perished completely in a great storm for abandoning monotheism, were also Nephilim. Eventually, the Anunnaki gods became enraged and, using gravity technology, redirected one of the meteors that were rapidly moving through the sky towards Planet Earth.

Recently, researchers have discovered a pit that is 30 kilometres (18.5 miles) in diameter in the Indian Ocean. This pit, which is located 1,500 kilometres (932 miles) southeast of Madagascar, is the exact site where the meteor hit the Earth's surface, according to researchers. This meteor is probably the same size as the meteor that caused the extinction of dinosaurs 65 million years ago, a meteorite with a diameter of 13 kilometres (eight miles). Such a meteor is said to have the power of five billion Hiroshima atomic bombs. The resulting blast from this collision created a mega-tsunami with waves hundreds of metres high that battered the surrounding land for countless hours. At the same time, a magnitude 12 earthquake was underway. These catastrophic events occurred soon after the meteorite hit the Earth. It was shattered into millions of tiny fiery boulders. Then those fiery boulders entered the atmosphere until a shower of fire and ash fell upon the earth and scorched the Earth's forests. The Earth had become hell. As a result of this rain of fire from the sky and the burning of the forests, Earth's temperature rose so much that all the water of the seas, rivers, and all the ice on the Earth covering a huge area of the northern hemisphere for 2.5 million years suddenly evaporated. After that, it rained for 40 days and nights until the entire surface of the Earth was covered with water, and no living beings had a chance to escape. Even the tall Nephilims had no chance of surviving after 40 days and nights of rain. It took almost as long to drain that amount of water. This was the end of the Ice Age after 2.5 million years on Earth.

Recently, geologists have discovered a layer of ash several centimetres deep that can be found all over the world. In addition, fossils of marine animals can now be seen in all countries of the world. Archaeologists have recently claimed they have found the remains of a giant ship near the top of Mount Ararat in south-eastern Turkey. They have discovered layers of fossilized animals, such as elephants, penguins, fish, palm trees, and thousands of plant species at this site.

Moreover, these fossils, which mainly include animals from tropical and cold regions, show that the bodies of these animals and plants remained under the mud and turned into fossils after the water receded. There are also the remains of over a million graves surrounding Noah's Ark. Over 10,000 years ago, people from all over the world buried their dead in this area, believing that being close to God's chosen would also lead to their salvation.

Before Noah's flood, there were civilizations, like Atlantis in America, Göbekli Tepe in Turkey, and Gunung Padang in Indonesia. Gunung Padang is the name of an ancient place of worship in West Java, Indonesia. This place of worship consists of a series of stone steps leading to the top of a hill. But this hill was originally a four-layered artificial pyramid, and each of these layers was built at specific times. The outermost layer dates from 3,500 years ago. The second layer was built 8,000 years ago. The third layer 9,500 years ago, and the oldest layer, the first one, dates back to 28,000 years ago.

Göbekli Tepe in south-eastern Turkey is an ancient complex of a series of pillars with intricate designs, some weighing as much as 10 tons. The history of the area dates back to 2,000 B.C., while its crumbling columns, said to have collapsed at the end of the Ice Age, testify to its destruction because of a great flood. In December 2000, the remains of an ancient civilization were discovered just off the coast of India in the Gulf of Khambhat by the National Institute of Ocean Technology. This underwater city dates back to 30,000 B.C. In addition, the lost city of Atlantis, dating back to more than 10,000 years B.C., had the most advanced civilization on the planet and eventually went underwater and disappeared due to a big flood. The existence of such advanced ancient civilizations, dating back tens of thousands of years, is evidence of the occurrence of a great global flood at the end of the last Ice Age.

After the flood of Noah, humans entered a 5,000-year dark age. Although no significant civilization arose during this period, the first significant human civilizations arose in Mesopotamia afterwards.

The fact is that Noah's Ark had a limited capacity for these thousands of animal and plant species. Even collecting all these pairs of animals was very difficult for Noah. The main purpose of the Anunnaki gods in ordering Noah to gather pairs of animals and various types of seeds and plants was to enable him and his family to continue living and producing offspring after the great flood had subsided. Although animals, such as cows, sheep, chickens, roosters, bees, and plant seeds, such as wheat, barley, corn, and rice are essential for human survival, this limited number of animal and plant species was not enough to revitalize life on Earth. Therefore, the extraterrestrial gods collected genetic samples from all kinds of animals and plants and preserved all these samples in a gene bank in a spaceship, and after the great flood receded, they used them to restore animal and plant life on Earth.

Noah himself was a human-alien hybrid. His father, Lamech, always blamed Noah's mother, Betenos, for Noah's unnatural appearance. It is said that Noah had glowing skin, and her eyes glowed in the dark like the eyes of animals. Noah's father often asked his wife if she had ever had sex with one of the Anunnaki gods and if Noah was a combination of alien and human. Noah and his grandfather, Methuselah, both lived long lives. Methuselah lived 969 years on Earth, and Noah lived for 950 years. They were both human-alien hybrids and therefore had luminous bodies and lived long lives. But Noah and Methuselah weren't the only people who lived long lives. Apparently, humans lived long after the great flood was over. In addition, giants such as Gilgamesh and Goliath lived at that time. Goliath was the commander of the Philistine army in the war with the Israelites, who was killed by the prophet David.

GILGAMESH

Gilgamesh was the king of the ancient city of Uruk in Mesopotamia. He used to destroy all the wedding ceremonies in the town. He stole the bride and made love with her before she could embrace her future husband. To punish him, the goddess Ishtar created a creature called Enkidu. Enkidu lived in the underworld where predators and evil creatures lived in chaos. After Enkidu was neglected by the goddess Ishtar, the animals and creatures of the underworld got angry at him, so he went to the human world. There, he met Gilgamesh and challenged him to a fight. The two warriors fought a bitter battle on the streets of the city. However, Gilgamesh won the battle, and both eventually became inseparable friends. His friendship with Enkidu made Gilgamesh more compassionate than before. No longer interested in the new brides of Uruk, he decided to use his supernatural powers in war. These two friends embarked on a six-day journey to the Cedar Forest, where they met and fought with Humbaba, the guardian of the forest. Eventually, Gilgamesh killed Humbaba by delivering the final blow to him.

After this, they returned to their own city of Uruk. Meanwhile, the goddess Ishtar took an interest in Gilgamesh, but Gilgamesh rejected her with unkindness. In retaliation, Ishtar unleashed the Bull of Heaven to go to Uruk and kill the people and destroy the houses there.

Gilgamesh and Enkidu fought this creature and defended the city. They were able to kill the Bull of Heaven, which provoked the wrath of the gods against them, and they killed Enkidu in retaliation. The death of Gilgamesh's friend, Enkidu, was a turning point in his life because he did not believe in death until that moment in his life. But, eventually, he realized that there is a great truth called death from which no living being can escape. Enkidu died and travelled to the underworld where the dead knelt and ate ashes.

Gilgamesh was very depressed at the death of his friend. He was afraid that one day this story could happen to him, too. Finally, Gilgamesh went to the high mountains to find the secret of eternal life. He walked through the rocks and different areas, through the extreme cold and the scorching sun, until he finally reached the end of the world. There was a small café there that served drinks.

The manager of this café was a goddess named Shiduri. The goddess told Gilgamesh to stop making such a strange request because all creatures are doomed to die, and they should enjoy life until death comes. Gilgamesh did not accept her words. Shiduri told him, 'Take this way. Cross the waters of death, and you will meet a man named Utnapishtim (Noah). He is an immortal man and has come alive out of the Great Storm.'

So, Gilgamesh built a large ship, put a pair of each kind of animal in it and sailed the way that Shiduri showed him. He met Utnapishtim at the top of a mountain. Utnapishtim also told Gilgamesh that all creatures will one day face death. But Gilgamesh still didn't want to accept that fact. Utnapishtim told him that if he could overcome his sleep, the gods would give him eternal life. Gilgamesh was able to stay awake for seven days and nights but finally fell asleep on the seventh night. This time, Utnapishtim said,

'There is a magical plant in the ocean. This plant can give you eternal life.' Gilgamesh was able to find the plant on the seabed, but on the way to land, a serpent stole the plant from him. Finally, Gilgamesh returned to his city. He felt that he had come to terms with death. And now the thought of dying didn't bother him anymore, and he vowed to spend the rest of his life doing good deeds.

MITHRA (MITHRAS)

Mithra (Mithras), the god of kindness, the sun, justice, the oaths, and the keeper of livestock, crops, and water, is one of the most important mythological gods and predates Ahura Mazda (the god of Zoroastrianism) and has many followers around the world. God Mithras sent Ahura Mazda to guide and teach the Persians, who, like the Egyptians before them, were polytheistic, and Ahura Mazda taught Zoroaster his doctrines to guide the Persians.

Mithraism contains the mysteries of the Zodiac constellations, the upper worlds, stargates, Apocalypse, and the eye of providence. After Persia, Mithraism gradually became popular in ancient Rome. Altogether, Mithraism had seven stages. The people who entered it, when they passed all seven steps, would attain the rank of master and were called the sons of Mithras. At the same time, when they reached the rank of Mithra's sons, they became aware of some confidential information about the system of creation and the universe, heaven, hell, and the day of judgment.

According to some of these mysteries, the jury at the Bridge of Sarat (Chinood) – where the souls of the deceased are judged and their good and bad deeds, merits and sins are weighed – consists of three gods: Mithras, Soroush, and Rashen. Rashen holds the Minoy scale, which never makes mistakes and doesn't stray by even a hair's breadth for the rich or poor. In the end, it is God Mithra who determines which level that each pure, semi-pure, evil, and semi-evil soul should be placed on and their position in Heaven, Hell, or on Earth.

In Greek mythology, Cerberus, often referred to as the hound of Hades, is a many-headed hound that guards the gates of the underworld to prevent the dead from leaving. The Gospel of Matthew (2:1-12) speaks of sages or wise men who followed a star from the east to Bethlehem in search of a newborn king. There, they found Mary and the baby Jesus and offered him gold, frankincense, and myrrh. These three wise men belonged to the group of The Sons of Mithras. After Christ's physical resurrection, Mary Magdalene, who was closest to Christ in his lifetime, boarded boats with her family members to a town called Saintes-Maries de la Mer on the southeast coast of France while being protected by Mithras' 72 sons. From there, the sons took Mary and her family to the Sainte-Baume cave. Because of the deep emotional relationship between Jesus and Mary Magdalene, it is assumed that she was the wife of the Messiah and even carried the Christ child in her womb during this journey. Thereafter, the work of spreading Christianity was begun by Maximinus Ax, one of Christ's close disciples in the area.

After losing to Maxentius at the Battle of the Milvian Bridge, Constantine the Great suddenly saw a luminous object, in the shape of a cross, in the sky. He then swore that if God would help him win the battle, he would convert to Christianity and replace Christianity with Mithraism, which was then the Roman religion. And finally, it happened. After winning the battle, Constantine became the Roman Emperor and began to suppress the followers of Mithraism and replace Christianity as the official Roman religion. From then on, the followers of Mithraism were forced to worship the god in secret.

In 1244, the church ordered the massacre of the inhabitants of a village belonging to the Cathar sect. The Cathars believed that the official church had deviated from its path since the time of Pope Sylvester I. They wanted to follow the message of Christ and ignored the Earthly world and the mortal body of man. The Cathars believed in the existence of two gods, one good and one evil, which was one of the reasons for the Catholic Church's enmity with the Cathars. The Catholic Church claimed that this contradicted monotheism, a fundamental principle that there is only one God who created all things visible and invisible. Well, the Cathars were right in this regard.

Most ancient civilizations believed in the existence of multiple gods. For example, the Mesopotamian Sumerians believed that heaven was ruled by a god named Anu and the Earth by a god named Enki or Enlil. The ancient Egyptians also believed in other gods, like Ptah, Shu, Tefnut, Geb, Nut, Osiris, Isis, Anubis, and Horus while worshipping Ra (Re) as the creator of the universe. Also, the ancient Greeks worshipped dozens of gods, such as Zeus, Poseidon, Apollo, etc. In addition, the ancient Hindus worshipped three main gods, Brahma, Vishnu, and Shiva. The Cathars believed that the good god (the god of the New Testament) was the creator of the spiritual kingdom, while the evil god (the god of the Old Testament) was the creator of the physical world, and many Cathars believed that he was Satan. The Cathars believed that human spirits are actually asexual spirits of angels trapped in the material realm of the evil god and destined to constantly incarnate on Earth until they attain salvation. The Cathars' only ideological error was that they misidentified Satan. In fact, whether in heaven, purgatory,

Earth, or hell, the Anunnaki gods all work together towards a common goal, which is to administer the affairs of creation. The only devils to interfere with this path are other extraterrestrial beings of non-human races, depicted in the Bible as beings with two horns. These interdimensional aliens are powerful and plan to dominate and corrupt the spirits of humans with the aim of overthrowing the human race and occupying the territory of the Anunnaki gods on Earth.

But, alas, the church of the time, unaware of the mysteries of Mithras and under the influence of these otherworldly demons, began to suppress and kill the Cathars, who belonged to the sons of Mithras. Part of the mysteries of Mithra, which its followers attain in the seventh stage, is actually the knowledge and ability to communicate with the higher worlds. This technique is also common in Hindu Buddhism and among the Mayan, Aztec, and African tribes and is often performed by ascetics and humans. This was usually done by inhaling the vapours of certain types of plants or consuming marijuana or drinking the infusion of certain herbal remedies. After that, the person would fall into a trance state and could open a stargate to higher dimensions by generating negative energy and thus communicate with extraterrestrial demons living in the upper worlds. Pythia, oracle of the Temple of Apollo at Delphi, sat on a chair that was on top of a hole, and, after inhaling the steam escaping from this hole, she entered a trance state and could predict future events. Her predictions included the defeat of the Greeks at the Battle of Thermopylae against the Persians and the massacre of 300 Spartan warriors.

ALEISTER CROWLEY

Aleister Crowley was born on October 12, 1875, to a wealthy and religious family in England. His parents were fanatical Christians. As a result, Aleister was engaged in Bible studies starting from an early age. But, after a while, when Aleister Crowley reached puberty, he began to explore the thoughts and ideas of his own family. He changed his name from Alexander to Aleister to show his disapproval and was always happy to be called by that name.

In 1903, Crowley married a girl named Rose Edith Kelly. They travelled to Egypt for their honeymoon. In Egypt, Crowley learned about summoning spirits. At the time, Rose, Crowley's wife, announced that she received messages from one of the ancient Egyptian gods named Horus. When they returned from Cairo in 1945, Rose, who until then had no idea about magic, often fell in a trance. She told her husband that God was trying to communicate with her. To test his wife, one day, Crowley took her to a museum to identify the image of Horus among a large number of images of Egyptian gods. To his surprise, she was able to correctly identify the image of Horus. This painting belonged to an old family. In this image, Horus was receiving sacrifices from the dead.

In his childhood, Crowley had believed that his special number was 666, and, when he realized that the image of Horus was in the row of 666, Crowley took his wife's words seriously. While no one was allowed to enter the Great Pyramid of Egypt, which is one of the most energetic points on the planet, Crowley entered it one night and sat in a triangular shape at the centre of the pyramid while wearing a triangular hat. So, due to the geometric similarity, he was able to gain more energy. At the same time, a blue spirit named Aiwass appeared to him and dictated to him some instructions from the ancient Egyptian gods. Then, Crowley published these instructions as *The Book of the Law*. This book mentions the signs of Satanism and the things that please Satan.

In 1904, Aleister Crowley went to the Great Pyramid of Giza in Egypt and performed satanic rituals for 40 days and nights, worshipping and praising Satan. In 1904, on April 8, 9, and 10, a spirit named Aiwass appeared to him and introduced himself as Satan's prophet and told Crowley that he had been chosen by Satan to be the prophet of the Apocalypse. Aleister Crowley said, 'I played the role of the prophet, Aiwass played the role of Gabriel, and Satan played the role of God.'

According to Crowley, Satan's instructions were given to him in three chapters, and he wrote these instructions in a book called *The Book of the Law*. This book, which contains Satan's instructions to his followers and predicts the future, has been hidden for years. But in today's times, on the anniversary of Crowley's visit to the Great Pyramid of Giza, Freemasons gather around each other and perform satanic rituals by dancing naked around the pyramid and making sacrifices. The purpose of the Masons in these actions is to create a stargate by creating negative energy. Negative (dark) energy is the best factor to open a stargate and travel to other worlds. The more negative (dark) energy, the easier it is to communicate with other dimensions. Our universe is created in the form of intelligent energy, and this energy was proved by Albert Einstein in the theory of relativity: $E = mc^2$. Every human body is made up of atoms and electrons, and these particles are connected all over the universe.

As a result, every action we do and even everything we think affects the entire universe. Therefore, the human body continuously emits energy to the environment. By performing satanic rituals around the Great Pyramid of Giza, the Freemasons release one of the greatest dark energies and negative forces into space, and as a result, a stargate opens through which they can summon alien demons from higher dimensions. Jinns also enter the Earth the same way. In fact, summoning spirits by creating and opening and stargate is one of the most important knowledges of the Illuminati and Freemasons, who are part of the Sons of Mithras sect.

The appearance of Aleister Crowley can be considered a turning point in the development of witchcraft and Satanism in the West. The establishment of sexual debauchery with music and the use of magical drugs caused him to be called the greatest devil and the lowest person on Earth. Edward Aleister Crowley was an English occultist, prolific writer, ceremonial magician, pleasure seeker, rock climber, chess fan, sexual revolutionist, and social critic. He is perhaps best known today for his writings on occult sciences. His famous masterpiece, *The Book of the Law*, which was dictated to him by a possibly incorporeal being called Aiwass, was the basis for a religious and philosophical system he called Thelema. He played an important role in several witch cults, including Golden Dawn and Astrum Argenteum.

Infamous during his lifetime, Crowley was called the meanest man in the world.

In 1898, at the age of 23, Crowley met a man named George Cecil Jones. Jones was a member of a society called the Golden Dawn where people seemed interested in learning magic. This association was completely secret and was founded by Samuel Liddell McGregor Mathers. In this secret society, Crowley was able to learn the sciences of alchemy, occultism, astrology, and other things.
It is interesting that, during this period, prominent people, such as William Butler Yeats, who was one of the leading British poets, and Arthur Edward White were also members of this secret society. Combining the essence of Theravada Buddhism with Vedantic yoga and ritual magic, this association researched, practiced, and taught magical and mystical methods, as well as scientific enlightenment.

Crowley decided to join this association that year and was able to develop rapidly and make significant advances. He was influenced in this regard by Allen Bennett. Bennett left England in 1899 and immigrated to Ceylon to join Buddhist temples.

THE PRIORY OF SION

In 1956, a fraternal organization called the Priory of Sion was officially founded by Pierre Plantard. However, the organization later stated that it was founded in 1099 as a secret organization on Mount Zion in Jerusalem by a historical monastic group called the Abbey of Our Lady of Mount Zion whose mission was to study the historical secrets of the Cathars (or Mithra's Protection Secrets). The Priory of Sion was founded by a historic group of monks. In fact, they were the children of those three wise men who were present at Jesus Christ's birth, and it was these men who brought Mary Magdalene to Jerusalem and then took on the task of protecting her. They were the Sons of Mithras, later known as the Priory of Sion. It is stated in the ancient texts that the knowledge of Mithraism is a set of special sciences in the fields of astronomy and the heavens, which gives special abilities to its followers.

As Jesus Christ said: **'I know wonders that seem to violate the laws of physics and nature, although they are only performed to send a message to humanity.'**

And members of the Priory of Sion say: **'Jesus Christ wanted to prove that everyone can perform these miracles. We usually recognize it as having three components: soul, spirit, and consciousness. Through their evolution and harmony, man can ascend to God.'**

People who saw themselves as enemies of humanity, or in other words, as slaves of 666, or the devil within, always tried to destroy this ancient ritual. The members of this group, called masons, did so because of their knowledge; that is, they brainwashed them. However, some of these people, with the help of the teachings of the Sons of Mithras (or the Priory of Sion), returned to their former ways and were called Freemasons. Famous people, like George Washington, Benjamin Franklin, Franklin D. Roosevelt, Mark Twain, Oliver Hardy, Alexander Pope, Leonardo da Vinci, Wolfgang Mozart, and Thomas Edison were also Freemasons. Freemasons therefore followed the teachings of the Sons of Mithras (or the Priory of Sion), i.e., Mithraism.

THE EYE OF PROVIDENCE

The Eye of Providence is a symbol that shows an eye set in a triangle surrounded by rays of light or glory. This eye is meant to show divine providence and the importance of the eye of God watching over humanity. In modern times, the most prominent image of the Eye of Providence is on the reverse side of the Great Seal of the United States, where it says he Department of the Treasury, which is depicted on the United States' $1 bill. In Freemasonry, the Eye of Providence represents the eye of God that is always watching over humanity and reminds us that the thoughts and actions of a Mason are always under God's control. In Freemasonry, God is often mentioned as the Great Architect of the world. The Eye of Providence depicted on the $1 bill represents the influence that Freemasonry had in the founding of the United States.

THE THIRD EYE

A mysterious light that the shaman suddenly feels within himself. An inexplicable searchlight. A glowing fire that allows him to be able to see through the darkness even with his eyes closed, which helps him see things and upcoming events that are hidden from others.

The Third Eye, also called the eye of the spirit or inner eye, is a mystical invisible eye usually located on the forehead and offers insights that go beyond the normal vision. The Third Eye refers to a gateway that leads to the inner realms and spaces of higher consciousness. In spirituality, the Third Eye is often a symbol of the intellectual state. The Third Eye is often associated with religious insight, clairvoyance, the ability to observe the afterlife, and connection with other dimensional beings and out-of-body experiences. People who are said to have a Third Eye are sometimes referred to as psychics.

In Hinduism and Buddhism, the Third Eye represents enlightenment that comes via meditation. Hindus also wear a tilak on their foreheads as a symbol of the Third Eye, which is also seen in images of Shiva. Buddhists regard the Third Eye as the eye of consciousness, which is the point of receiving light beyond one's physical sight. In Taoism and many traditional Chinese religious sects, such as Chan, Third Eye training involves focusing on the point between the eyebrows with the eyes closed while the body is in various postures, such as Qigong. Qigong is a system of coordinated postures and movement, breathing, and meditation. In this case, people are aligned with the correct vibration of the universe and are given a solid foundation to reach a more advanced state of meditation.

The symbol of the Third Eye is the fruit of the pine tree, which can be seen on the Pope's staff and outside the Vatican. It is small and made up of pineal and interstitial cells and is located deep in the brain (midbrain) and between the right and left cerebral hemispheres. This gland produces a hormone called melatonin and a chemical substance called serotonin, and the secretion of these hormones is the highest at night and around noon. It is also related to the daily sleep-wake cycle. Shaped like the fruit of a fir tree or an eye, the pineal gland is actually the seat of the soul in the body. Opposite of the Third Eye is the human penis, which is a symbol of Earthly and material pleasure. Whenever a person has sex, his Third Eye is completely closed. In this case, the person's overall connection with spirituality and higher dimension is lost. This situation is very critical and dangerous. A person may commit bad deeds due to the loss of his spiritual vision and insight. This is also why a person feels self-loathing after sex. Sexual intercourse separates people from their extraterrestrial nature, i.e., the upper world (realm of angels), and turns their hope of salvation and return to eternal nature into despair.

MURAQABAH (MEDITATION)

Humans can never reach higher dimensions with Earthly technology and science.

Even with the most advanced UFOs that move at almost the speed of light, this is not possible. Perhaps in the future, humans will be able to physically travel between dimensions by obtaining detailed information from stargates, but currently humans only have access to spiritual ascension through meditation and meditation. Meditation, muraqabah, or introspection is actually the ability to work with the mind. Meditation is a practice in which a person uses a method, such as mindfulness or focusing the mind on a specific object, thought, or activity, to develop attention and awareness and achieve a smooth, calm, and mentally stable state. The main goal of meditation is to increase awareness and willpower so that you can use your mind to understand yourself, gain better control over your mind and body, and access higher intelligence. All these eventually translate into personal growth, leading to more relaxation, improved quality of life, and interaction with the environment.

Since the sexual organ is on the opposite point of the Third Eye, for spiritual ascension to higher dimensions, one must turn one's back to all worldly desires and pleasures, including food and water, even sleep and all thoughts related to the Earthly world. Forgetting material pleasures is possible only with willpower, which requires a strong mind. We should meditate to increase our willpower. The most important principle in meditation (yoga) is to focus on one point.

Gradually, through the spiritual practice of yoga, one can master the mind and thoughts and have the necessary willpower to take the spirit out of the prison of the body and elevate it to higher dimensions.

YIN AND YANG

Everything in this world has its opposite; for example, day and night, ugly and beautiful, hot and cold, far and near. In Taoism, there are two symbols called yin and yang. The white part is yang, and the black part is yin. Opposite points in the form of yin and yang means that when yin reaches its maximum and wants to end, it contains yang, and when yang wants to reach its maximum, it contains yin. That is, when one ends, another grows in it, and this cycle continues.

So, when we are happy within ourselves or our place in the world or even our home and any other place where we feel happy, Yin and Yang are considered to be at their most balanced. The main goal of meditation is to establish this balance and ultimately create peace and harmony.

Everything has its opposite. But yin and yang are not absolute opposites. They depend on each other. Taoism believes that the universe is full of different types of energy and vibration that act in different ways in different situations. Everything can be yin and yang. For example, the wheat you plant is yang, and the time you harvest it is yin. The crest of the wave is yang, and its bottom is yin. The gas pedal is yang, and the brake pedal is yin. The eggshell is yang, and its contents are yin. Yang is tougher, stronger, smarter, and faster, but both can be two sides of the same coin. Sun rays are yang compared to shadows. Throwing is yang and catching is yin. Yang initiates and yin perceives the movement. Yin is the space inside the glass, but yang is the glass itself. The warmth of coffee is yang, and its blackness is yin. Yang is male and yin is female. The water flowing slowly in the river is yin, but when it reaches the waterfall it becomes yang. A toothpick is yin compared to a lightning rod, and the human head is the yang part of the body. One of the main ideas of Taoism is the belief in the balance of power or yin and yang. These ideas represent pairs of opposites, such as light and dark, hot and cold, action and inaction, that work together and form a universal whole. Yin and yang show that everything in the universe is connected, and nothing has meaning alone.

Taoism teaches that all living things must live in a state of harmony with the universe and the energy within it. Ch'i, or Qi, is the energy that exists in the universe and guides everything in the world. Taoists believe in spiritual immortality in which the spirit of the body joins the universe after death. Tao is not a thing or substance in the traditional sense. It is not noticeable, but it can be seen in the affairs of the world. Although it produces all existence, it does not exist itself.

Tao has two faces. Unlike other religions where the supreme power is a good being with a purely evil rival, Taoism says we should learn from yin and yang. Taoism does not have personal gods. According to Taoism, when we move in the same direction as the harmony of the universe, we no longer have to fight the natural forces of the universe.

Taoism teaches us to listen more and talk less. We need to support or cancel something so that we can grow faster. It is not important to be the best; we must be who we are. It is better to just live because the luxuries and complications of life distract us from the Tao. Taoists also believe that a wise person is flexible.

Throughout human history, the power of the West and the power of the East have both maintained the balance of human forces ruling the Earth. For example, the Romans, who were the dominant power in the West, fought continuously for 700 years with the Persians, the superpower of the East. Currently, there are two superpowers in the world that are responsible for maintaining the balance of power. In the West, the United States and the European Union; and to the East, Japan, South Korea, and their allies. The presence of two superpowers in the world is always necessary because, as in the world of politics, when one superpower is formed, the presence of another superpower (an opposing force) gives the world a more democratic character. Otherwise, the ideas of totalitarianism, capitalism, bigotry (racial and religious), and communism would be more prevalent in the world. As China, India, Indonesia, Brazil, and other populous countries of the world occupy a large part of the global economy market and subsequently consume more resources and fossil fuels, this, in turn, leads to more pollution of the environment and atmosphere. In addition, the spread of the coronavirus from China, followed by the Russian military attack on Ukraine, and the occurrence of floods and droughts, as well as the migration crisis, and worst of all, the emergence of nationalist ideas and the spread of xenophobia in the world have harmed the world order. But its restoration requires the tolerance and cooperation of all the countries of the world, especially the populous countries that are the main consumers of the Earth's resources and consequently the main polluters of water, soil, atmosphere, and environment.

In fact, the philosophy of yin and yang in Taoism is quite correct because not only was white energy released after the big bang, but at the same time, another type of energy called dark energy was released into the depths of infinite space. Stars, planets, nebulae, and generally everything that can be seen in the physical dimension, whether with the naked eye or with the aided eye, constitutes only 5% of the volume of our material world. Although white energy creates the structural elements of all these cosmic bodies, it is known that about 68% of the universe is made up of dark energy. In addition, dark matter makes up about 27% of the universe's volume.

Dark energies and forces are always present throughout the universe. Human and animal bodies also release their own energy. The type and quality of energy that our body releases depends on our mindset. So, when we think positively, our body in turn releases waves of positive energy that bring security, peace, and progress to the environment. On the other hand, war, destruction, insecurity, poverty, and natural disasters (such as floods and earthquakes) result from negative energies caused by the world's imbalance; fights and family conflicts are the result of negative energies caused by the disturbance of the mind. When we remember the bitter memories of the past and our minds are filled with hatred and enmity, we unintentionally reflect our negative energies to the environment around us, and as a result, evil forces gain power on Earth. The more chaotic our thoughts, the less powerful the positive and divine forces will be against the evil forces.

'When the sinners are organized and
the comet appears, the Roman Empire will rise,
and you and I will die there. He will rise from
the raging sea and out form an army
at every corner. He will throw brother upon
brother to destroy mankind.'
Book of Revelation

666

Extraterrestrial demons have always existed throughout human history and have tried to deceive and enslave
humanity with trivial toys. Human enslavement by extraterrestrial demons usually revolves around the four
factors of power, fame, wealth, and lust, i.e., the same
things that prevent the spiritual growth and ascension
of humanity and its return to its eternal and angelic nature. Extraterrestrial demons have entered the world of
politics, business, art (music, cinema), and sports, especially football, to achieve this goal. If you look closely,
you can see that the Satan symbol appears in some famous brands in the world. For example, the number 666,
which is a special number for Satan, appears in the famous Walt Disney logo or in the Google Chrome logo,
which contains three 6s in each other. There is also a
number 666 hidden in the Vodafone brand logo. You
can see the image of the Melosine mermaid on the famous logo of the Starbucks chain's coffee shops, but if
you turn it upside down, the image of a horned animal
appears. In addition, the Hebrew number 666 is clearly
visible in the Monster Energy Drink's logo. And dozens
of other companies around the world all have satanic
symbols in their logos.

Today, there is a barcode on all the products we buy.
This barcode consists of a series of parallel lines, called
bars, that are spaced from each other. Each line of these
barcodes represents a specific number written below the

same line. Each specific product has its own barcode, and each barcode has a series of numbers that is unique and not similar to any other product. From the series of numbers in the barcode, only three 6s are fixed while the remaining numbers are variable. Two of these 6s are at the beginning and end of the barcode, and the other is in the middle. Today, people in many countries around the world can pay for goods by placing their thumb on a biometric sensor and don't even need to carry a bank card.

Bible Revelation Chapter 13, Section 16, refers to Satan's takeover of power before the Apocalypse, and all people, great and small, rich and poor, white and black, must have a mark on their right hand so that no one can do business without having the mark on their right hand, which is either the name of Satan or the number of his name.

'It also compelled all men, great and small, rich and poor, free and slave, to make a mark on their right hand or on their foreheads so that they could not buy or sell without having the mark, that is the name of the beast, or the number of its name. That requires wisdom. Let the discerning person calculate the number of the beast, for it is the number of a man. That number is 666.'
Book of Revelation 13:16-18

The body carries the spirit, but the nature of the spirit is different. Unlike the body, which belongs to the Earth, the human spirit is a gift from God. The pure spirit does not belong to this Earthly dimension, so at the moment of death, it is released from the prison of the body and immediately returns to its original home, heaven, to live with other pure spirits in a world without pain and suffering. Only sin-tainted spirits reincarnate in new bodies on Earth after death or go straight to hell. However, when the spirits of sinful extraterrestrial angels lose their place in heaven, they are banished to the prison of Planet Earth or, worst of all, go straight to hell. Because of the material and sinful nature of the physical world, they are constantly subject to sin. However, it is very difficult for them to return to the higher dimension after that, and they are often reincarnated in different bodies on Planet Earth or even reborn in hell. But this is not the whole story because even the spirits of sinful angels, after their exile to the physical world, are divided into different groups, depending on the amount and type of sins they have already committed in their previous lives. Therefore, the quality of life of exiled souls or fallen angels on Earth is different. In other words, all humans, whether we live on Earth or in hell, are fallible. Even the lives of angels and pure spirits who live in heaven are not guaranteed. Any flaw, any mistake can eventually lead to their fall from heaven to the physical world. Christ, the bearer of the Spirit of God, came to lead mankind. Today, Christianity is the enemy of evil thoughts and the support and guide of man on the way to reach his luminous and divine essence.

'O Father, we praise your name in heaven.
O great Lord, who owns the earth and time,
give us your blessings. Forgive the wrongdoers
as we forgive those who oppress us. Keep us from
falling into the trap of Satan's lusts and tempta-
tions. Save me, O Lord. Guide me in your name with
your power. Zealous men have risen up against me.

Cruel men try to kill me.
But God is with me.
He will save my life. God is always my support.
Greetings and praise to father and son. As it was
from the beginning, so it will be now.
The world has no end. The Lord is like a strong
fortress. He protects me from my enemies.'
Letter to the Romans

Basically, one should beware of talking to the devil. Except for the necessary questions, any kind of conversation with the devil is dangerous. Satan mixes truth with lies. One should not listen to Satan. Satan's deception has a psychological aspect. Satan is a liar by nature. He lies to mislead us. Satan is strong. But we bear the burden of life not for Christ, but for ourselves. Life is a platform to test human nature. While only the purest natures deserve to live in heaven, the rest are condemned to end their lives on Earth or the underworld. Christ knows human instincts. He sets the rules so that they stand against each other. Then it awakens the instincts in people. Look at it, but don't touch it. Touch it, but don't taste it. Taste it, but don't swallow it. For Satan, the kingdom of the underworld is better than serving in heaven. Satan was present in all human miseries on Earth from the beginning. Unlike Christ, Satan cultivates every emotion that man likes. He gives him what he wants; he never judges him. Why? Because Satan never rejects a person with all his faults and shortcomings. Satan is man's guardian. Satan is a philanthropist. Perhaps the last true philanthropist. Who can deny that the whole 20th century didn't belong to Satan? All of it. Satan is on the alert. Because it's the devil's turn. Laws are what we live by. Rules: The law is the last entrance and the newest style of priests. But this is how Satan is defeated. Satan is doomed. Right to choose; it's true.

> **'I know the miracles that seem to violate
> the laws of physics and nature [were] created
> only to convey a message to humanity.'**
> *Jesus Christ*

And members of the Priory of Sion say Jesus Christ wanted to prove that anyone can perform these miracles and that we humans are made up of three components: spirit, consciousness, and body, which, through their coordination and development, can ascend from the human to the divine.

PSYCHOSIS

Have you ever heard of psychosis? Psychosis is an abnormal mental state that results in problems determining what is real and what is not. Symptoms can include delusions and hallucinations. Additional symptoms include incoherent speech and behaviour that is inappropriate for a particular situation. Donald, Donald, look what God has made! He is one of those special creatures of God. The new millennium has just begun. He bounces back and forth like a baseball with every step. Donald, look closely at him for he is a prime example for the people of this millennium.

The appearance of such people is not strange at all. When the inherent characteristics of people are so excited that they wish to swallow the world, when the selfishness of the people becomes as big as the churches, the world must adapt to them. Then, this peaceful relationship will continue until each person builds an empire for himself and even becomes his own god. But do you know what happens next? As man's greed continues, who can control it from above? The world will reach a stage when the air will become heavy and the water acidic. Bee honey also becomes radioactive. There is nothing to stop here. And there is no time to think or prepare. Man has sold his future so much in advance that there is no future for him. Now he's looking for a way out.

But now millions of Vladimir appear, and each of them is ready to destroy his world alone. Then they lick their fingers. Even after that, they send bills for trash like themselves. It's time to pay back, Vladimir! Now is the time to pay for the evil deeds of your past. You can't escape from this swamp anymore, Vladimir! With full bellies that have milked everyone and with bloodshot eyes, they scream and ask for help. But do you know where the problem comes from? There is no one to help! You are alone now, Vladimir! You were once an example of the best creations of God! Do you know who is to blame?

EXORCISM

Today, most world leaders have a group of people in their employ who, like shamans, are able to communicate with extraterrestrial demons using special methods. Apparently, these people achieve this power through long periods of austerity and the use of marijuana or water lotus or drinking the combined decoction of several special herbs and doing yoga exercises in a state of high concentration. During this process, the exorcist intentionally opens a stargate to the upper dimension, thereby communicating with extraterrestrial gods and demons. Exorcists are able to predict some future events by consulting these evil spirits that appear only to them. Some of the leaders of the Eastern governments even ask these exorcists to cast spells on other governments and enemy countries or to undo the spells placed on them by these rival governments.

THE ARMAGEDDON

Just before Christ appears in the end times, Satan becomes a geopolitical force in the world, going to world leaders and summoning a united army of all nations. Then he goes to war with God's army in Megiddo plain, 17 kilometres (10.5 miles) from Jerusalem. In this battle, the army of angels of Jesus Christ, with their fiery weapons from the air and the ground, engage with the army of Satan and destroy them. After Christ's victory over Satan, suddenly a voice from the holy sky announces the end of the world. At this moment, a very strong earthquake shakes all the cities, plains, and mountains. Fifty-kilogram (110-pound) hailstones start falling from the sky and destroy everything.

> 'Here is wisdom. Let him that hath understanding count the number of the beast: for it is the number of a man; and his number is six hundred threescore and six.'
> *Book of Revelation 13:18*

> "Then I heard a loud voice from the temple saying to the seven angels, 'Go, pour out the seven bowls of God's wrath on the earth.' The first angel went and poured out his bowl on the land, and ugly, festering sores broke out on the people who had the mark of the beast and worshiped its image. The second angel poured out his bowl

on the sea, and it turned into blood like that of a dead person, and every living thing in the sea died. The third angel poured out his bowl on the rivers and springs of water, and they became blood. Then I heard the angel in charge of the waters say: 'You are just in these judgments, O Holy One, you who are and who were; for they have shed the blood of your holy people and your prophets, and you have given them blood to drink as they deserve.' And I heard the altar answer: 'Yes, Lord God Almighty, true and just are your judgments.' The fourth angel poured out his bowl on the sun, and the sun was allowed to scorch people with fire. They were seared by the intense heat, and they cursed the name of God, who had control over these plagues, but they refused to repent and glorify him. The fifth angel poured out his bowl on the throne of the beast, and its kingdom was plunged into darkness. People gnawed their tongues in agony and cursed the God of heaven because of their pains and their sores, but they refused to repent of what they had done. The sixth angel poured out his bowl on the great river Euphrates, and its water was dried up to prepare the way for the kings from the East. Then I saw three impure spirits that looked like frogs; they came out of the mouth of the dragon, out of the mouth of the beast and out of the mouth of the false prophet. They are demonic spirits that perform signs, and they go out to the kings of the whole world, to gather them for the battle on the great day of God Almighty.

'Look, I come like a thief! Blessed is the one who stays awake and remains clothed, so as not to go naked and be shamefully exposed.' Then they gathered the kings together to the place that, in Hebrew, is called Armageddon. The seventh angel poured out his bowl into the air, and out of the temple came a loud voice from the throne, saying, 'It is done!' Then there came flashes of lightning, rumblings, peals of thunder and a severe earthquake. No earthquake like it has ever occurred since mankind has been on earth, so tremendous was the quake. The great city split into three parts, and the cities of the nations collapsed. God remembered Babylon the Great and gave her the cup filled with the wine of the fury of his wrath. Every island fled away, and the mountains could not be found. From the sky, huge hailstones, each weighing about a hundred pounds, fell on people. And they cursed God on account of the plague of hail, because the plague was so terrible."

Book of Revelation 16:1-21

THE APOCALYPSE

The physical world, that is, the world before our eyes, has countless natural gateways to the higher dimension. Some of these natural stargates that exist on Planet Earth are found inside caves and some others are found in mountains and historical places. Natural stargates in space are mostly found in the Pleiades star cluster and the Orion Belt, while Sirius itself is a natural stargate. But the most important of them, which I have dubbed the Mother Stargate, is the stargate through which Lord Mithras descended to the Planet Earth from the higher dimension on December 24, 9678 B.C. After the spread of Mithraism around the Earth, the god Mithras not only changed the direction of the Earth's axis by deflecting a celestial meteor towards the Earth, but she also caused a great global flood. As a result of this great global flood, the Earth's temperature increased and caused the sudden melting of all the ice on this planet. And this was the end of the ice age.

Have you ever really looked at Leonardo da Vinci's Last Supper painting? In this painting, Jesus Christ is seen sitting at a table with 12 of his apostles. Six of the apostles stand on the left and six on the right of Christ. Each of these apostles is a symbol for one of the zodiac constellations. The zodiac is divided into 12 signs, each occupying 30 degrees of celestial longitude and roughly corresponding to the following astronomical constellations: Aries, Taurus, Gemini, Cancer, Leo, Virgo, Libra,

Scorpio, Sagittarius, Capricorn, Aquarius, and Pisces. Earth's axis moves one degree every 72 years compared to the stars and constellations of the zodiac, which is known as the global year. This means that the zodiac signs rotate 360 degrees around the Earth every 25,920 years. In traditional archaeology, the zodiac is known as the celestial dome.

In our physical world, which is controlled by the Anunnaki Gods, there are only eight main stargates to the higher dimension, and all other stargates, whether natural or artificial, are all secondary. However, the space aliens use the same sub-stargates to reach these eight 'mother' interdimensional gateways. One of these eight main stargates is more important than the others. And this stargate is placed between the constellations Sagittarius and Libra every 25,920 years. And, 11,700 years have passed since the end of the last Ice Age, which ended due to the great flood (Noah's flood). As a result of this flood, life on the Planet Earth was almost destroyed, so it can be called an Apocalypse. But when is the next Apocalypse date? On September 8, in 14,220 A.D., the two constellations of Sagittarius and Libra will be parallel with the three stars of Orion's Belt, the Pleiades (Seven Sisters), Sirius, and the Great Pyramid of Giza. On this day, the sun stands over the Great Pyramid of Giza for a few minutes. On September 8, in 14,220 A.D., the eighth 'mother' stargate opens for a few minutes as it lies between Libra and Sagittarius, and this is the exact date of the next Apocalypse.

THE SPIRIT

But what is the nature of the spirit? What is it really? According to some, it is the manifestation of human desires. But the spirit flies to God, like a voice that vanishes into the air. The Greeks say the same. Their philosophers believe that life is death. However, the Incas were sun worshippers. The reason was atmospheric factors. Those who lived in the mountains died from the cold at night. The sun is the absolute ruler of the sky. They died without sun. The Incas who lived on the coast worshipped a minor goddess called Mama Quila (Moon Mother). Children were sacrificed on a bed of wool and cotton. Not only the children, but even when the chief of a tribe died, it was customary to bury his wife with him at the funeral ceremony – his wife and the best wife he loved, also a large number of servants, jewels, silverware, horses, weapons, food, and clothing. So, in their philosophy, death was life.

However, Viracocha, Inti, and Mama Quilla were the three main gods and goddesses of the Incas. Pacha Mama was also a goddess worshipped by the Incas. The Incas believed that she was an Earth mother and a fertility goddess who guided planting and harvesting. Mama Quilla was the wife of the sun god and moon mother in Inca mythology and religion. She was the older sister and wife of Inti, daughter of Viracocha, and mother of Manco Cápac and Mama Uqllu, the mythical founders of the Inca Empire and culture.

The ancient Egyptians believed that the soul consists of many parts. In addition to these components of the soul, there was also a human body. According to ancient Egyptian creation myths, the sun god, Atum, used his magic to create himself, other gods, and the entire universe from chaos. Since the Earth is made of magic, the Egyptians believed that the world and all its living beings were imbued with magic. When humans were created, this magic took the form of the soul, an eternal force that resides in and with every human being.

Egyptians had a special ceremony to bury pharaohs. After the death of a king, his body was embalmed and placed in a coffin. The coffin was then placed in a pyramid along with some magical curses, plenty of food and drink, furniture, clothes, and jewelry. Finally, they sealed the door of the pyramid so that no one could enter. The way after death was long, and that is why the Egyptians buried their dead with food, water, and wine. Archaeologists discovered the remains of six wine jars and eight fruit baskets in Tutankhamun's tomb. In order for the pharaohs of Egypt to be able to travel to the afterlife adorned, they buried their jewelry and clothes with them. Tutankhamun has more than 50 costumes in his tomb, including shirts, tunics, handkerchiefs, gloves, and wigs. Also, there are several bracelets, necklaces, pendants, and buckles, all made of gold. On top of all that, there is gold, jewels, and precious stones in his tomb. To avoid the heat of the grave, hand fans were also buried with him. One of these hand fans is made of elephant ivory and ostrich feathers. Another piece of equipment needed by the pharaohs in the world after death was the boat! Next to Pharaoh Khufu, who built the largest pyramid of Giza as his tomb, stands a large ship about 45 metres (147.5 feet) long. Some archaeologists believe that this was a solar chariot so that the king could travel across the sky with the sun god Ra. Although there is no boat in Tutankhamun's tomb, 12 oars are buried with him. Perhaps he did not like the boat, because three chariots and about 130 pieces of ivory, silver, gold, and ebony were discovered in his tomb. The favourite perfumes and oils of the Egyptian pharaohs, all made of the most expensive materials, were usually buried with them. When archaeologists excavated Tutankhamun's tomb, one of his perfumes was still in a marble bottle. Tests have shown that this perfume is made from coconut oil and frankincense.

Various types of weapons were found in Tutankhamun's tomb. This was done mainly for personal defence during possible dangers in the king's afterlife. But sometimes these weapons were buried next to the dead just for show. Some of these tools found in Tutankhamun's tomb appear to have never been used before. Large shields and golden chariots were among the items that had to be placed in smaller pieces in the tomb due to their usually large size. Some of them may have been the favourite war weapons of King Tut. Flying sticks (something like a boomerang) were also seen in the tomb of this Egyptian king. Archaeologists believe that they were used to hunt birds in the afterlife.

Ancient Egyptians believed that the soul is made up of three parts: Ka, Ba, and Akh. Ba refers to the personality of the deceased person that remains in the living world – the physical essence after death. BA has traditionally been depicted as a falcon with a human head. The idea behind this bird-like thing was that the Ba would fly out of the deceased's grave every morning and affect the world of the living throughout the day. Every evening, the Ba would fly back to the grave and rejoin the body of the deceased person for the night. It is also believed that the Ba was one of the reasons for the practice of mummification. Mummies, their graves, and often just statues of the deceased when their bodies could not be recovered, were intended to help the Ba find the remains of the deceased each evening. The Ka was essentially a person's double. It was the life force and was separated from the body at death. The reason for the extensive and elaborate preparation of the body for the afterlife was to ensure that the Ka had a home. The living sometimes provided bread, beer, oxen, and fowl to feed the Ka for the afterlife. They also believed that, in order for the Ka to recognize its body, the deceased body had to be as similar as possible to the previous living body. If possible, the living would leave more than food for the deceased. They also left servants, weapons, jewelry, clothing, and their mummified pets in their graves – anything that would aid them in their afterlife. Akh is the spirit of Re who embodies the concept of light that had transfigured the spirit of a person who becomes one with the light after death.

The opposite of Akh is courage (dead), the state of a person who has died but has not been turned into light. In order to become an Akh, humans had to be assimilated and transformed into this new state. Only after the bodies of the dead had been embalmed and properly buried, and only after the spirits of those dead had survived all the obstacles of death and the trials of the underworld, could they attain salvation.

REINCARNATION

Reincarnation, or Samsara, is a mystical belief in which the spirit begins a new life in another body after biological death. Resurrection is a similar process postulated in some religions where the spirit is resurrected in the same body. In most reincarnation beliefs, the spirit is immortal, and only the body can die. After death, the spirit is transferred to a new baby (or animal) to live again. In Jainism, a soul travels into each of the four states of existence after death, based on its karma. The heavenly state (the highest state of existence), the human state, the animal state, and the hellish state (the lowest state of existence).

Reincarnation in Hinduism refers to the cycle of life and death, the transfer of the spirit from a dead body to a new body, and the repetition of the cycle of birth and death. According to Hinduism, this cycle continues until the spirit is cleansed of impurities, neglect, and ignorance. Imagine going somewhere you've never been. Suddenly, you look to the side and come across an accident scene. You hear cars speeding past you, and you see the shadows of people passing by. You feel like you have experienced these things elsewhere.

Many people believe that they lived in a different time, in a different society, and in a different body. This stage of death and rebirth is called reincarnation. The Dalai Lama has claimed that a young boy is the reincarnation of a spiritual leader. A woman remembers things from her past life and tries to find the children of her past life. It is difficult to explain reincarnation from a scientific point of view.

In June 1972, Carol gave birth to her second child. She and her husband named the child Ilya. The doctors said the delivery was easy. The only strange thing was the baby's feet. Carol noticed the baby's legs when she held her for the first time. His legs were in a strange shape as if they were stretched. It was as if he was always sitting. The doctor explained that this complication is normal and can be fixed with a simple surgery. The child's family believed in Buddhism and thought it might be a sign of something else. When Ilya was two years old, his family moved to Montreal and opened a Buddhist centre there. When Ilya was eight years old, the Dalai Lama told him that he was the reincarnation of a Buddhist monk named Tenzin Sherab. The child was not surprised by this, but his family was sceptical.

Carol and her husband believed in reincarnation but were emotionally disturbed because their son belonged to another world. They wanted their son to grow up with them, but Tibetan leaders claimed the child as theirs. For several years, the family corresponded with Tibetan leaders. They wanted their son back. Only when the Dalai Lama asked Tenzin to join them did the family relent. Tenzin was only 14 years old at that time. It was the hardest decision his mother had ever made. In October 1986, Carol and her husband decided to give up their son. Tenzin and his mother made their way to the monastery, where 25,000 monks lived. Tenzin felt comfortable among the monks because he had not travelled alone. Tenzin knew the place he was in from the dreams he had seen before. The monks claimed that Tenzin was very similar to Geshe

Jatse. Within months, Tenzin learned the Tibetan language and memorized the scattered manuscripts, as well as began to practice Buddhist rites. Determined to discover the truth, Tenzin meditated constantly. According to Tibetan Buddhists, reincarnation is a normal thing. Western scientists study and explore outer space. They also study the spirit and power of the human mind. The mind doesn't work like a video camera, which means we can't record our experiences. Instead, these memories are stored in the innermost layers of our mind, allowing us to easily recall these memories in different situations. Although we can remember what we did in the past, we don't know when or where we learned those memories. So, we must have learned all this somewhere before.

An English woman is sure that she once lived a different life. Jenny Cockell was born in 1953 in Barnet, Hertfordshire. She laments the nervous pressure she suffered as a child and remembers the agony of the moment of death. She often had these dreams at night, but these memories also tormented her during the day. In her youth, she remembered her past life memories both in sleep and wakefulness. These pictures had nothing to do with her future. They were reminders of the moment of death in her past. Cockell's most vivid and lasting memories of her past life were those of a poor, working-class woman in Ireland named Mary, who had eight children before her death. Her first memory of Mary's death in the hospital was in a recurring dream she first talked about when she was three. Gradually, she remembered the events on her deathbed more clearly and told her mother that she felt great guilt for abandoning her children to an unknown fate. Cockell's dreams included her experiences after Mary's death. She knew she was dead and felt her consciousness leaving her body, as she viewed her body from a perspective about 10 feet above her and slightly to the side. She saw a nurse pacing around the room and saw a person, whom she first believed to be Mary's husband but later realized he was a priest, entered the room and knelt by her bed. Suddenly, she was pulled from behind by a stretcher. She was sucked into a narrow tube and then into a dimly lit room, where she sensed the presence of other spirits.

As a child, Jenny would draw in front of the fireplace. She painted a picture of a two-room cottage, a woman with a child, a soldier, and a dock. And she also drew a map of a town called Malahide in Ireland. Jenny's mother said: 'I think she was six or seven years old at the time. She drew a map and said it was a city where she used to live, and she just didn't know exactly where that city was now. She said the town was very small and also had a river.' Jenny's mother became increasingly suspicious after hearing her daughter's words. She thought it was just childish behaviour, but she was still suspicious.

Jenny kept telling the same stories over and over again. Jenny told stories about her eight children. She even knew their names, personalities, and faces very well and was always worried about them. As Jenny grew older, her memories slowly faded. She wanted to go to Ireland to find her missing children, but she was sure that her family would not take her to Ireland. After getting married and having children, she began to examine her past memories. In 1980, Jenny took one of the maps she had drawn as a child to a bookstore. The bookseller told her that the map she had drawn was of the city of

Malahide. She later went to a hypnotist to find out more. Jenny said: 'After I went to the hypnotist, all the memories came back to me. I couldn't ignore them anymore, and I was tired. I had decided to go to Ireland.' However, Jenny had to take care of her children and did not have enough money to go to Malahide.

Finally, nine years later, she was able to go there. This town was 14 kilometres (8.7 miles) northwest of Dublin. First, she found the pier and then the church she thought she had attended as a child. And then she found the ruins of what she believed to be her former home. Everything there went according to the plan she drew as a child. Jenny said: 'It was wonderful to be in Malahide. The whole time I was there, I remembered all the old memories. I was sure that I had returned home.' Jenny was just starting her research. She found out that a woman named Mary Sutton had lived in that house in the past. After Mary's death, the children were placed in an orphanage. And some of those children were still alive. And Jenny decided to find the kids. A little later, she found herself with a family who had lost their mother 60 years ago. Jenny Cockell began to believe that she was reminiscing about a woman named Mary who lived in Ireland. She had eight children and died in 1932. Reminiscing about her childhood, Jenny rediscovered where Mary lived. And now she was determined to find all the children of Mary. She advertised in newspapers. She wrote to all the new houses in the area and tried to find people with this surname. And finally, she succeeded in reaching her goal. Eventually, she found Mary's eldest son, Sonny. In 1990, she had a brief telephone conversation with Sonny, Mary's eldest son, who was then 71 and lived in the north of England.

This led to a face-to-face meeting at his home, where he confirmed the accuracy of her memories of his mother. The people, the buildings and surroundings, the daily concerns and activities, and special incidents were all correct. Among other things, Sonny Cockell confirmed Mary's impression of that cottage, which had been the lodge of Gaybrook house – the colour of the exterior walls, which were sometimes whitewashed; the pronounced depression in the roof; the colour of the exterior walls, which were sometimes whitewashed; the layout of the rooms; the stove in the kitchen fireplace with a hob on both sides and a hook on the chimney for pots; and the vegetable patch. Sonny agreed that the appearance and personality of each of the children was just as Cockell remembered them, along with her memory of Mary wearing a blouse, a calf-length wool skirt, and a shawl. Sonny revealed that Mary's husband, John Sutton, had worked as a scaffolder, which explained the impression that he was busy with large beams as well as roofing work. John was an outsider in the sense that he wasn't from the area, and, although he was British and not Irish, he had served in the Royal Dublin Fusiliers and fought in the First World War. Jenny was the reincarnation of Sonny's mother. The memories fitted Mary's life.

Finally, Jenny's puzzle was put together. She had decided to find the rest of her children. She researched further, and Sonny helped her a lot. Eventually, she found five of her children. After 60 years of separation, the family was reunited.

Another reincarnation case is the case of an Indian girl named Shanti Devi. Shanti Devi (December 11, 1926 – December 27, 1987) told her family at the age of four that she was married and had a husband and children somewhere nearby. But her parents didn't take her seriously. Disappointed with her parents, she tried unsuccessfully to go there at the age of six. Shanti also told her story to the teachers and the principal of the school. When the headmaster spoke to Shanti, the headmaster remarked that Shanti often used words from the Mathura dialect, so the headmaster thought maybe Shanti was talking about the village of Mathura. Eventually, the headmaster went to Mathura to look for Kedar Nath, the alleged husband of Shanti Devi. The headmaster was able to locate a businessman of the same name who had lost his young wife nine years and 10 months after their child was born. The case was even brought to the attention of Mahatma Gandhi, who set up a commission of inquiry. The commission travelled to Mathura with Shanti Devi. There, she recognized several family members from her previous life, including Lugdi's grandfather. Eventually, the commission concluded that Shanti Devi was, in fact, the reincarnation of Lugdi.

Apparently, a limited number of righteous people, who had succumbed less to their animal instincts than others during their material life, returned to their luminous and angelic nature and finally reach eternal life. On the other hand, those people who have not achieved salvation, depending on the percentage of blackness of their souls, are reborn in the form of humans or animals on Earth to have a second chance to atone for the sins of their past lives. The quality of life of each of these sinful souls is different depending on the amount of sin they had committed in their previous life. Siddhartha Gautama, also known as the Buddha, once drew a circle with a piece of red chalk and said:

'When men, even unknowingly,
are to meet one day, whatever may befall each,
whatever their diverging paths, on the said day,
they will inevitably come together in the red circle.'

Now we, all captives of the Holy Lord, are gathered again in the red circle. However, the only way out of the red circle or physical matrix is to turn our backs on the world and give up material pleasures.

NIRVANA

Nirvana is a concept in the Indian religions (Hinduism, Buddhism, Jainism, and Sikhism) that represents the ultimate state of spiritual peace, which is the result of attaining Moksha, or liberation, from the cycle of rebirth (Samsara). Nirvana is a place of perfect peace and happiness, like heaven. It is the highest spiritual state that the spirit can reach. The state of enlightenment is when all of a person's desires and sufferings completely disappear. Nirvana is the ultimate goal, the end of all spiritual journeys. It's like we're forever connected to another dimension that normal people can't understand. Those who have experienced it and are still alive usually do not like to share this experience with others. According to Indian religions, breaking the cycle can be achieved by detaching from the sense of self and merging or absorbing into the higher world. These religions consider the higher world as an indescribable world without physical dimensions, space, and time. In yoga philosophy, breaking the cycle of Samsara is explained by transcending human awareness of time and space and cause and effect.

According to Buddhist thought, nothing in the world of Samsara is real. In fact, the existence of this cycle is rooted in the wrong belief in its concept, which is actually an imaginary belief. When man reaches enlightenment, or Nirvana, he speaks from his unconscious. He says that I have a name, a personal history, many memories, and dreams, but if we look closely, we see that these are just illusions. 'I am now looking for something that is no longer hidden from me.' The "I" freed from mental images. Just like a raindrop connecting with the ocean and a cloud disappearing in the sky. When Siddhartha came to this realization, he became Buddha.

> **'I take the earth as a witness to my liberation from the cycle of life and death. Wow! This light is the nature of all people. However, people suffer from its lack and are caught in the endless and illusory cycle of Samsara.'**
> *Siddhartha Gautama (the Buddha)*

According to Buddhists, Parinirvana is the final stage of Nirvana that occurs with the death of the enlightened being's physical body. The moment when the Buddha was finally able to free himself from the endless cycle of life and death (Bhava Chakra). According to Indian religions (Buddhism, Hinduism, Sikhism, and Jainism), rebirth takes place in six realms, namely three good realms (Heaven, Demigod, Human) and three evil realms (Animal, Ghost, Hell). Samsara ends when one attains Nirvana, casts out desires, and gains true insight into the impermanence and reality of the non-self.

RESURRECTION

In the year of 33 A.D., 40 days before Jesus' crucifixion, Jesus called Peter, James, and his brother, John, and took them with him to the top of a high mountain. When they reached the top of the mountain, Jesus was transfigured before them, his face shining like the sun and his clothes were as white as snow. Suddenly, Moses and Elijah appeared to them and spoke to him. Then Peter said to Jesus, 'Lord, it is good for us to be here. If you want, I will build three mansions here, one for you, one for Moses, and one for Elias.' While he was still talking, suddenly a bright cloud overshadowed them, and a voice from the cloud said, 'This is my beloved Son, with whom I am well pleased. Listen to him.' When the disciples heard this, they fell to the ground, overwhelmed by fear. But Jesus came and touched them and said, 'Get up and don't be afraid.' And when they looked up, they saw no one but Jesus himself. As they were going down the mountain, Jesus commanded them, 'Don't tell anyone about the vision until the Son of Man is raised from the dead.' Forty days after this incident, the Romans arrested Jesus and crucified him. Then on Friday, a rich man named Joseph of Arimathea buried the body of Jesus Christ in a tomb in the Garden of Calvary. When Mary Magdalene and the other women went there on Sunday to anoint the body of Jesus, they saw that the great stone had been moved away from the tomb. So, they went into the tomb and saw a young man sitting on the right side.

His clothes were shining white. They were amazed. The angel said to them, 'Do not be afraid! I know that you are looking for Jesus, who was crucified. He is not here! He has risen from the dead, just as he said would happen. Come and see where his body was lying. Then go quickly and tell his disciples that he has risen from the dead and is going ahead of you into Galilee. There you will see him.' During the Mass ceremony, the participants embody the spirit of Jesus in the church. The way it works is that the participants in the Mass unwittingly open a stargate to the higher dimension by singing religious hymns. The spirit of Jesus enters the church through the same stargate and reincarnates in the bodies of people whose vibration of the quantum energy strings is in harmony with the vibration of the quantum energy strings of the Holy Spirit.

**'When two or three are gathered in my name,
I am in their midst.'**
Matthew 18:20

The secret is that by standing side by side, people aimlessly create a suitable platform to receive the great energy of the Holy Spirit with their bodies. So, they are actually bringing Jesus Christ to life. In fact, the resurrection of the Holy Spirit is similar to the phenomenon of being possessed by evil spirits. The only difference is that people possessed by evil spirits align the energy vibrations of their body with the energy vibrations of the evil spirits. This phenomenon usually occurs when people cultivate evil thoughts in their mind and reflect waves of negative energy into the environment. As a result, these people are quickly identified by dark forces and evil spirits. By occupying these people's bodies, the evil spirits control their will, thereby inciting them to do evil deeds. So, one of the methods of communicating with extraterrestrial spirits is the coordinated performance of group hymns. This frequency emits a special sound into space, which then causes an interdimensional gateway to open. All the spirits of extraterrestrial beings, both benevolent and evil, use these stargates for interdimensional teleportation.

Elijah was a prophet and miracle worker who lived in the northern kingdom of Israel during the reign of Ahab (9th century B.C.). Elijah defended the worship of the Hebrew god over the worship of the Canaanite god Baal. God also performed many miracles through Elijah, including the resurrection, bringing down fire from the sky and entering heaven alive through fire. Elijah's remarkable rise during his lifetime, like Enoch before him, inspired the belief that God must have a special plan for Elijah. In Malachi 3:24, we read, 'Behold, I send Elijah the prophet unto you before the terrible day of the Lord cometh.' In Jewish tradition, Elijah is expected to be the herald of the Messiah. John the Baptist (born in the 1st century B.C., died in 28-36 A.D.) was a Jewish prophet of the Jordan region, celebrated by the Christian church as a forerunner of Jesus Christ. He emerged from the wilderness, preached a message of repentance for the forgiveness of sins, and offered water baptism to confirm the penitent's commitment to a new, sin-cleansed life. However, throughout history, some prophets, like Elijah, Christ, Moses, Abraham, etc., were able to do extraordinary things that caught mankind's attention. For example,

Moses' rod could turn into a serpent. Elijah, wearing a special belt around his waist, laid himself three times on the body of an old woman's son, and, after praying to God, the lifeless body of this boy came to life.

When Elijah and Elisha were on their way from Gilgal, suddenly a chariot of fire and horses of fire appeared and separated the two, and Elijah went up to heaven in a whirlwind. Elisha saw this and cried out, 'My father! My father! The chariots and horsemen of Israel!' And Elisha saw him no more. Healing the blind, raising the dead, and predicting the future were also among the miracles of prophets, like Jesus Christ.

Now these questions are raised here: Did the miracles and supernatural actions of these prophets really have no scientific and logical basis? Weren't these prophets actually mystics who, through their austerity and seclusion, possessed a kind of transcendental connection with beings of other dimensions?

If we examine the history of these prophets, we will see that most of them spent at least part of their lives in caves and deserts, meditating, and austerity. Likewise, Hindu ascetics and Mesoamerican tribal shamans communicate with extraterrestrials living in other dimensions. Apparently, these were extraterrestrial beings who informed the prophets of future events and enabled them to perform otherworldly tasks, such as raising the dead, healing the blind, turning a wand into a dragon. Also, it was these extradimensional beings who helped Moses provide food for his people during their 40 years of wandering in the Sinai desert. Are all these wonders really nothing but some advanced technologies beyond human understanding? And for this reason, don't these extraterrestrial beings seem holy and divine to us? Aren't divine angels actually advanced extraterrestrial beings that can travel between dimensions? Isn't Dajjal, who appears before the Apocalypse and takes an external form, actually an extraterrestrial devil?

When the Roman Empire rises, the Antichrist will appear and rule Solomon's Temple in Jerusalem. Meanwhile, Elijah and Enoch appear and herald the coming of the Messiah. Dajjal kills both of them, but by the will of God, they are resurrected after three days. Then the world will plunge into the darkness of injustice and great chaos. While God will shorten those days for the sake of righteous people, the Antichrist will be killed by the Archangel Michael at the will of God on the Mount of Olives.

> 'The dragon stood on the shore of the sea. And I saw a beast coming out of the sea. It had 10 horns and seven heads, with 10 crowns on its horns, and on each head a blasphemous name. The beast I saw resembled a leopard but had feet like those of a bear and a mouth like that of a lion. The dragon gave the beast his power and his throne and great authority. One of the heads of the beast seemed to have had a fatal wound, but the fatal wound had been healed. The whole world was filled with wonder and followed the beast. People worshiped the dragon because he had given authority to the beast, and they also worshiped the beast and asked, "Who is like the beast? Who can wage war against it?" The beast was given a mouth to utter proud words and blasphemies and to exercise its authority

for 42 months. It opened its mouth to blaspheme God, and to slander his name and his dwelling place and those who live in heaven. It was given power to wage war against God's holy people and to conquer them. And it was given authority over every tribe, people, language and nation. All inhabitants of the earth will worship the beast – all whose names have not been written in the Lamb's book of life, the Lamb who was slain from the creation of the world. Whoever has ears, let them hear.

"If anyone is to go into captivity,
into captivity they will go.
If anyone is to be killed[c] with the sword,
with the sword they will be killed."

This calls for patient endurance and faithfulness on the part of God's people.'
The Book of Revelation 13:1-10

In The Book of Revelation, there is a description of the events that will take place around the second resurrection of Jesus and after that. During the Great Tribulation, everyone will experience worldwide hardships, persecution, disasters, famine, war, pain, and suffering, which will affect all of creation, and precede judgment of all when the Second Coming takes place. However, those who choose to follow God will be raptured before the tribulation, and thus escape it.

The New Testament says that Christ will come to Earth before the Great Tribulation and take all true believers, living and dead, to heaven. During these sufferings and wars, the believers are in heaven and Christ fights with the people of Israel against the Antichrist. Only those Christians who do not truly believe in Christ and commit evil deeds will be alive during the Great Tribulation and will have to endure great suffering and pain. The Tribulation is thought to occur before the Second Coming of Jesus and during the End of Time. In this view, the Tribulation will last seven years in all, but the Great Tribulation will be the second half of the Tribulation period. The Antichrist (Dajjal) will appear in the world at the End of Time and establish an evil hegemony on Earth. He is a powerful and cruel ruler who pretends to be God and performs miracles. From the Christian perspective, he still lives on Earth.

Don Piper is one of the most interesting examples of resurrection. On January 18, 1989, Baptist minister Don Piper was involved in a horrific car accident on his way home. When paramedics arrived, they found no signs of life in Piper and covered him with a tarp. Ninety minutes later, when he was taken to the hospital, he revived and claimed to have seen heaven and met his deceased relatives there. According to Piper, he went straight to heaven after passing out and experienced things he describes as amazing and beautiful, including meeting family members like his grandmother and joining the heavenly choir while they were moving towards the gates of heaven.

BABA VANGA

Baba Vanga was a blind European fortune teller who correctly predicted the events of 9/11, Brexit, the collapse of the Soviet Union, the death of Princess Diana, the 2004 tsunami in Thailand, and the presidency of Barack Obama. She has also made other predictions about the rise in global temperature in the near future and its consequences. Baba Vanga predicted that in the future, the Earth will be so warm that people will build underwater cities to live there. Also, she has predicted the occurrence of natural disasters, such as floods, famines, earthquakes, tsunamis, wars, and migration, as a result of the planet's high temperature. The high temperature of the Earth will continue until the year 14,220.

Then, due to the impact of a meteorite with the Earth and the occurrence of a global flood, eventually civilization will completely disappear from the Earth. Only a small group of international astronauts living on the surface of the Moon and planets like Mars will survive this horrific disaster. After months of continuous rain, greenhouse gases are gradually washed out of the Earth's atmosphere and return to the Earth's surface.

Then, the conditions will be created for plants and animals to thrive, and human civilizations will reappear on Earth. But during this time mankind, will make great scientific and technological advances and will be able to build space stations and small cities on the surface of some planets and their moons, like the Moon,

Mars, Jupiter, Europa, etc. In other words, technological advances may destroy humanity at first, but ultimately, they will save it. But only the human body perishes, while the human soul is eternal. After the emergence of new human civilizations on Earth, the human population will increase again, so, over time, more physical bodies will be found for the souls of people who were drowned in the global deluge, and until then, these souls will be processed in purgatory.

THE GODS OF THE PERSIANS

50 kilometres (31 miles) northwest of Shiraz, there are the ruins of the ancient city of Persepolis, the capital of the Achaemenid Empire. This city was built by Darius the Great more than 2,000 years ago.

Persepolis was once a great city that was said to be protected by a powerful god named Ahura Mazda. On a stone at the site of the ruins of the Palace of the Three Gates, the image of the winged god Ahuramazda sits in the centre of a circle. Ahura Mazda is the name of the god and the lord of all existence in Zoroastrian religion. Although Ahura Mazda is considered the god of the Zoroastrian religion, he himself was sent by another powerful god named Mithras. For this reason, the roots of Mithraism come from the land of Persia.

The Zoroastrian religion is based on truth and goodness. Lies and impurity are strongly rejected in the religion. This principle can be seen in the prayer of Cyrus the Great, the founder of the Achaemenid dynasty and the father of Persian civilization, for the people of Iran.

'O Lord Ahura Mazda, great creator of this land, keep my land and my people from lies.'
Cyrus the Great

Also, good thoughts, good words, and good deeds are the three principles of Zoroastrianism. In the Zoroastrian worldview, the world is an arena of conflict between good and evil, and, in the end, good will triumph over evil. Many characteristics of Mazda worship – such as the belief in the coming of a Redeemer, free will, judgment after death, heaven and hell – later became core tenets of other philosophical schools, like Christianity, Judaism, Islam and Jainism, and also influenced Greek philosophy and Buddhism. Avesta is the name of the Zoroastrian scriptures. This book also contains the Gathas. The Gathas are 17 poems, which are the words of Zarathustra and contain his messages and teachings. Zoroastrian gods are divided into two categories. The first group are Ahuras (Anunnaki gods), and the second group are Ahrimans (alien demons), although demons are not worthy of worship.

Ahriman (Angra Mainyu) is the destructive and Evil Spirit in Zoroastrianism. He is the twin brother of Spenta Mainyu, the Holy Spirit, and both are the sons of Ahura Mazda, the wise lord and supreme god of Zoroastrianism. Ahura Mazda is the Creator God and maintains the order of the world with the light of truth and righteousness (Asha). Asha is actually some kind of alien weapon. In Zoroastrianism, people have the right to choose whether or not to accompany Ahura Mazda because the Zoroastrian religion holds humanity responsible for its choices. There is no force as strong as Ahura Mazda.

However, Angra Mainyu (the destructive spirit), which evolved from Aka Manah (the devil), is the main enemy of the religion and is opposed to Spenta Mainyu (the creative spirit). In Middle Persian literature, Angra Mainyu is mentioned as Ahriman, and he is the enemy of Ahura Mazda. Asha (truth and universal order) is the life force derived from Ahura Mazda and is opposed to Druj (falsehood, deception). Druj is the most powerful demon that captures humans. This demon and his followers are a big part of the demon army. Ahura Mazda is absolutely good, and there is no evil in it. He oversees gētīg (the material world) and mēnōg (the spiritual world), with the help of Amesha Spentas and other gods. They all worship Ahura Mazda, and Ahura Mazda designates them as worthy of worship in the Avesta. The ultimate purpose in a Zoroastrian's life is to become an Ashavan (a master of the Asha) and to bring happiness to the world because luck helps forces of good versus forces of evil. The main core of the Zoroastrian religion (Mazdaism) is summarized in its meaning to follow the triple path of Asha, which revolves around good thought, good speech, and good deeds (humata). Much emphasis is also placed on spreading happiness, primarily through charity, and respecting the spiritual equality and duty of men and women. From the perspective of the Zoroastrian religion, humanity's role in the world is to serve and honour not only the wise Lord, but also the seven blessed creations of air, water, soil, plants, animals, humans, and fire – the gifts of Almighty God to him. By helping to create a state of perfection in this world, Zoroaster required his followers to walk a moral and straight path. In addition, Avesta (the Zoroastrian holy book) and other ancient Zoroastrian texts call for the protection of nature, making it an ecological religion.

Developed centuries earlier by the prophet Zarathustra, this Persian religion spread throughout the empire. Zoroastrianism was the dominant faith of the Achaemenid Persian Empire. With a central belief in the supreme deity, Ahura Mazda, Zoroastrianism is perhaps one of the first true monotheistic religions.

THE ACHAEMENID EMPIRE

Basically, the Achaemenid Empire was founded by Cyrus the Great after the rise of the Zoroastrian religion in the 6th century B.C. Cyrus the Great had a royal lineage. He was the son of Kamboji I and Mandana. During his 30-year reign, he was able to expand the Achaemenid Empire from the east to India, the northeast to the Aral Sea, the north to Georgia, the northwest to Bulgaria, the west to Libya, and the south to Libya.

During this period, many countries and regions – including Egypt, Turkey, Pakistan, Afghanistan, Iraq, Syria, Jordan, Palestine, Lebanon, Israel, Bulgaria, Armenia, Azerbaijan, Georgia, Turkmenistan, Tajikistan, Uzbekistan, Kyrgyzstan, parts of India, the United Arab Emirates, Qatar, Bahrain, Kuwait, northern Saudi Arabia, and eastern Libya – were all part of the Achaemenid Empire.

Cyrus is also known for his achievements in human rights, politics, and military strategy, as well as his influence on Eastern and Western civilizations. After the conquest of Babylon, he facilitated the return of the Jews to Jerusalem.

According to Isaiah 45 of the Hebrew Bible, God anointed Cyrus for this work and even called him the Messiah in the sense of the word, Anointed One.

**'This is what the Lord says to his anointed,
to Cyrus, whose right hand I take hold of
to subdue nations before him**

and to strip kings of their armor,
to open doors before him
so that gates will not be shut:
I will go before you
and will level the mountains;
I will break down gates of bronze
and cut through bars of iron.
I will give you hidden treasures,
riches stored in secret places,
so that you may know that I am the Lord,
the God of Israel, who summons you by name.
For the sake of Jacob my servant,
of Israel my chosen,
I summon you by name
and bestow on you a title of honor,
though you do not acknowledge me.
I am the Lord, and there is no other;
apart from me there is no God.
I will strengthen you,
though you have not acknowledged me,
so that from the rising of the sun
to the place of its setting
people may know there is none besides me.
I am the Lord, and there is no other.
I form the light and create darkness,
I bring prosperity and create disaster;
I, the Lord, do all these things.

You heavens above, rain down my righteousness;
let the clouds shower it down.
Let the earth open wide,
let salvation spring up,

let righteousness flourish with it;
I, the Lord, have created it.

Woe to those who quarrel with their Maker,
those who are nothing but potsherds
among the potsherds on the ground.
Does the clay say to the potter,
What are you making?
Does your work say,
The potter has no hands?
Woe to the one who says to a father,
What have you begotten?
or to a mother,
What have you brought to birth?

This is what the Lord says –
the Holy One of Israel, and its Maker:
Concerning things to come,
do you question me about my children,
or give me orders about the work of my hands?
It is I who made the earth
and created mankind on it.
My own hands stretched out the heavens;
I marshaled their starry hosts.
I will raise up Cyrus in my righteousness:
I will make all his ways straight.

He will rebuild my city
and set my exiles free,
but not for a price or reward,
says the Lord Almighty.

This is what the Lord says:

The products of Egypt and the merchandise of Cush,
and those tall Sabeans –
they will come over to you
and will be yours;
they will trudge behind you,
coming over to you in chains.
They will bow down before you
and plead with you, saying,
Surely God is with you, and there is no other;
there is no other god.'
Isaiah 45

In March 1879, Assyrian archaeologist Hormuz Rasam found a cylindrical clay tablet during his excavations at the Babylon archaeological site. This clay cylinder, known as Cyrus the Great's Charter of Human Rights, is now kept in the British Museum. The text of this clay tablet reads as follows:

'I am Cyrus, King of the world, great king, mighty king, king of Babylon, king of the land of Sumer and Akkad, king of the four quarters, son of Camboujiyah (Cambyases), great king, king of Anshân, grandson of Kouroṣh (Cyrus), great king, king of Anshân, descendant of Chaish-Pesh (Teispes), great king, king of Anshân, progeny of an unending royal line, whose rule Bel and Nabu cherish, whose kingship they desire for their hearts, pleasure. When I well-disposed, entered Babylon, I set up a seat of domination in the royal palace amidst jubilation and rejoicing. Marduk the great god, caused the big-hearted inhabitations of Babylon to … … … … … me, I sought daily to worship him. At my deeds, Marduk, the great lord, rejoiced and to me, Kourosh (Cyrus), the king who worshipped him, and to Camboujiyah (Cambyases), my son, the offspring of (my) loins, and to all my troops he graciously gave his blessing, and in good sprit before him we glorified exceedingly his high divinity. All the kings who sat in throne rooms, throughout the four quarters, from the Upper to the Lower Sea, those who dwelt in … … … … …, all the kings of the West Country, who dwelt in tents, brought me their heavy tribute and kissed my feet in Babylon. From … … … … … to the cities of Ashur, Susa, Agade, and Eshnuna, the cities of Zamban, Meurnu, Der, as far as the region of the land of Gutium, the holy cities beyond the Tigris whose sanctuaries had been in ruins over a long period, the gods whose abode is in the midst of them, I returned to their places and housed them in lasting abodes. I gathered together all their inhabitations and restored (to them) their dwellings. The gods of Sumer and Akkad whom Nabounids had, to the anger of the lord of the gods, brought into Babylon. I, at the bidding of Marduk, the great lord, made to dwell in peace in their habitations, delightful abodes. May all the gods whom I have placed within their sanctuaries address a daily prayer in my favour before Bel and Nabu, that my days may be long, and may they say to Marduk my lord. May Cyrus the King, who reveres thee, and Camboujiyah (Cambyases) my son … Now that

I put the crown of kingdom of Persia, Babylon, and the nations of the four directions on the head with the help of God (Ahura Mazda), I announce that I will respect the traditions, customs and religions of the nations of my empire and never let any of my governors and subordinates look down on or insult them until I am alive. From now on, till God grants me the kingdom favour, I will impose my monarchy on no nation. Each is free to accept it, and if any one of them rejects it, I never resolve on war to reign. Until I am the king of Persia, Babylon, and the nations of the four directions, I never let anyone oppress any others, and if it occurs, I will take his or her right back and penalize the oppressor. And until I am the monarch, I will never let anyone take possession of movable and landed properties of the others by force or without compensation. Until I am alive, I prevent unpaid, forced labour. Today, I announce that everyone is free to choose a religion. People are free to live in all regions and take up a job provided that they never violate other's rights. No one could be penalized for his or her relatives' faults. I prevent slavery and my governors and subordinates are obliged to prohibit exchanging men and women as slaves within their own ruling domains. Such a traditions should be exterminated the world over. I implore to God to make me succeed in fulfilling my obligations to the nations of Persia, Babylon, and the ones of the four directions.'

Powerful Achaemenid kings, such as Cyrus the Great, Darius the Great and Xerxes, owed their strength and power to the help of gods such as Mithras and Ahura Mazda. They are the same extraterrestrial beings who came to Earth thousands of years ago to sow the seeds of civilization in the corners of the world and cause the growth and prosperity of humans.

Zarathustra's first encounter with the god Ahura Mazda took place on a cloud-covered mountain and immersed in a strange light. Throughout history, mankind has not achieved its knowledge and civilization alone, but extraterrestrial beings have played an effective role in creating many technological and cultural advancements of mankind. Usually, great inventors, physicists, mathematicians, soothsayers, and prophets, such as Nikola Tesla, Albert Einstein, Srinivasa Ramanujan, Pythias (Delphi Oracle), Michel Nostradamus, Baba Vanga, Jesus, Buddha, Moses, Elias, Zarathustra, Abraham, Joseph, and Enoch Smith, gained their knowledge either through direct contact with extraterrestrial beings or through Muraqabah (Meditation).

According to Buddhist legend, Maha Maya dreamed of a white elephant with six tusks penetrating her right side, meaning that she would give birth to a child who would become either the ruler of the world or the Buddha. However, aliens are said to be creatures with big heads, like elephants. Therefore, the elephant can be considered a kind of symbol of extraterrestrial beings. The mythological figure Merlin, prominent in the legend of King Arthur and best known as a magician, is said to have had no Earthly father, and his mother was conceived by an extraterrestrial being in her sleep. Merlin's alien father appears to be the source of all of his otherworldly powers and abilities. Noah's father, Lamech, always asked his wife if she had ever sex with any of the Nephilim or Anunnaki gods and if Noah was in fact the son of one of them because of Noah's lighter and brighter appearance. In Christianity, too, it is firmly assumed that Jesus Christ is the Son of God and that the divine spirit dwells in him. However, people who were half-human and half-divine have always been in contact with extraterrestrial beings and have been cared for and guided by the same extraterrestrials. In other words, these alien hybrids inherited their abnormal and extraordinary abilities from their alien fathers.

Akhenaten (meaning useful for Aten), was the pharaoh of ancient Egypt who lived between 1353 and 1336 B.C. Akhenaten chose this name for himself after his conversion to the Aten cult. Before his conversion, he was known as Amenhotep IV (meaning Amun is pleased). Based on the shape of Akhenaten's elongated skull seen on Egyptian hieroglyphs, it is believed that Akhenaten must have been a semi-alien being. Akhenaten always boasted about his strange and unnatural appearance. In all the hieroglyphs he left behind, Akhenaten is depicted with an elongated skull, a protruding abdomen, and chicken-like legs. Also, Akhenaten married his own sister, Nefertiti, to preserve his semi-divine lineage within the family. As pharaoh, Akhenaten is known for abandoning Egypt's traditional polytheism and introducing the monotheistic Aten religion. Since Akhenaten had ignored the gods of the Amun temple, the high priests of that temple cursed him so that he would never attain salvation, and, after his death, his soul would wander the Earth forever.

In 1907, Edward R. Ayrton discovered a mummy that could belong to Akhenaten in the Valley of the Kings. Genetic tests have shown that the mummy buried in tomb KV 55 belongs to Tutankhamun's father, Akhenaten. Freud suggested that Moses was a priest of Akhenaten who fled Egypt after the pharaoh's death and continued monotheism through another religion and was eventually murdered by his followers. Freud concludes that Moses was a follower of the monotheistic religion of Athens, but due to the weakening of imperial power after Akhenaten's death and during the post-Akhenaten uprisings, he was able to lead his followers to freedom, but they killed him after a riot and then joined another monotheistic tribe called the Medes.

Freud believed that years after Moses was killed, the Israelites repented and wished that Moses would return to save them again, so they invented the concept of a saviour. According to Freud, this feeling of guilt triggered by the killing of Moses was gradually passed on to the next generations and ultimately led to the birth of Judaism.

AKASHIC RECORDS

In a dimension beyond our dimension, all the information, memories, events, feelings, and thoughts of the universe's past, present, and future are collected, known as the Akashic records. With a thorough understanding of the knowledge of zero-point energy, one can enter this particular dimension and access Akashic memory through the opening of a stargate. Zero-point energy is the lowest possible vibrational energy that a quantum mechanical system, such as photons, electrons and quarks, can have. Quantum systems are constantly oscillating in their lowest energy state, and this phenomenon is called Quantum Oscillation. According to quantum field theory, the universe cannot be thought of as consisting of small discrete particles, but actually oscillating quantum fields are the building blocks of the universe. Matter fields whose quanta are fermions (such as leptons and quarks) and force fields whose quanta are bosons (such as photons and gluons) have zero-point energy. Recently, activities have been carried out at CERN in Switzerland to access the Higgs boson/particle. There, the world's leading scientists and physicists break apart electrons into their smallest components by accelerating beams of particles in the 27-kilometre (almost 17 miles) ring of the Large Hadron Collider (LHC). On July 4, 2012, scientists announced the observation of the Higgs boson, an elusive particle that gives mass to almost all other particles and, therefore, forms the basis of the matter from which we and everything we see in the universe are made. Accessing and gaining accurate knowledge of zero-point energy and the Higgs boson gives humanity the ability to travel to the farthest corners of the universe and black holes at near-light speeds. It is even possible that, with this knowledge, humanity will one day be able to travel between dimensions through the creation of artificial stargates. Interdimensional travel is possible only by penetrating the innermost layers of the universe, and quantum physics provides this possibility to mankind. In fact, the Supreme Power of the Universe has created this infinite world in the form of dimensions within each other. The whole Universe is actually made up of two dimensions. This is despite the fact that each of these dimensions includes two completely different worlds. As man is composed of two main parts, soul and body, the whole Universe is also composed of two dimensions, spiritual and physical. The spiritual dimension, which is the world of spirits, includes heaven and purgatory, while the physical dimension, which includes Earth and hell, is where sinful and semi-sinful spirits in human and animal bodies reside. Now, it is only through meditation that one can mystically ascend to the higher dimension and thereby attain Akashic memory.

Albert Einstein, a patent clerk in Switzerland, recalled how the idea of special relativity came to his mind at the age of 16 while chasing a beam of light. Einstein saw the light and achieved a kind of instant meditation that enabled him to ascend spiritually to the higher dimension and access the Akashic records. Unlike classical physics where time and space are intertwined, relativity justifies the creation of stargates and time travel to the past and future. Einstein was particularly interested in reading the book *Isis Unveiled: Secrets of the Ancient Wisdom Tradition*. This book is about human instinctive psychic ability and the hidden history of mankind. Michel de Nosterdam, a 16th-century French astrologer, physician, and soothsayer, is best known as the author of *Les Prophéties*, a collection of predictions of future events in poetic form. Nostradamus would usually go into a deep, meditative trance by staring at some water in a bowl. In this way, Nostradamus could access Akashic memory and supernatural information with instant spiritual ascension to the higher dimension. In the 16th century, soothsayers were condemned to be burned alive by the Inquisition for witchcraft. For this reason, Nostradamus published his collection of future predictions in the form of poetic quatrains in a book titled *Les Prophéties*. Nostradamus' prophecies were mysterious and poetic in a way that could not be understood until these prophecies were fulfilled. Among the prophecies of Nostradamus that came true are the following: The emergence of Louis Pasteur, the discoverer of germs; the atomic bombing of Hiroshima; The Great Fire of London; The Great French Revolution; the rise of Napoleon; the assassination of JFK and RFK; The death of Princess Diana and the explosion of the space shuttle Challenger. He also predicted the 9/11 attacks on the Twin Towers in New York City in the United States as follows:

> **'Earthshaking fire from the center of the Earth**
> **will cause tremors around the New City.**
> **Two great rocks will war for a long time,**
> **then Arethusa will redden a new river.'**

Nostradamus predicted the rise of Hitler as follows:

'From the depths of the West of Europe,
A young child will be born of poor people,
He who by his tongue will seduce a great troop;
His fame will increase towards the realm of the East.'

And

'Beasts ferocious with hunger will cross the rivers,
The greater part of the battlefield
will be against Hister.
Into a cage of iron will the great one be drawn,
When the child of Germany observes nothing.'

Furthermore, Nostradamus predicted that Charles de Gaulle would become the leader of France three times, and that's exactly what happened.

'Hercules become king of Rome and of Annemarc,
A man named De Gaulle is a three-time leader,
Italy and the waters of Venice will tremble,
He will be renowned above all monarchs.'

And regarding Louis Pasteur's discovery of microbes, he made the following prediction:

'The lost thing is discovered,
hidden for many centuries.
Pasteur will be celebrated
almost as a God-like figure.

This is when the moon
completes her great cycle,
But by other rumors,
he shall be dishonored.'

However, one of Nostradamus' most interesting prophecies relates to the death of Henry II:

'The young lion will overcome the older one,
On the field of combat in a single battle;
He will pierce his eyes through a golden cage,
Two wounds made one, then he dies a cruel death.'

It is obvious that, when one of the five senses or organs of the human body fails, the other senses or organs become stronger. Baba Vanga, the blind Bulgarian mystic and soothsayer who lost her sight in a storm as a child, claimed to have been contacted by beings from another world. She said that you don't see them now, but alien space shuttles are constantly moving through the sky. Baba Vanga claimed that, when she looked at someone, she could see all the events of his/her life, including the past, present, and future, like a movie. According to the researchers, so far, almost 80% of her predictions have come true. In 1980, the blind prophetess predicted that in August of 1999, Kursk would be flooded and the whole world would mourn. Kursk was a Russian nuclear submarine that sank in the Barents Sea on August 12, 2000, killing all on board. According to Baba Vanga, between 2025 and 2028, a new source of energy will be created, and world hunger will be eradicated from the face of the

Earth. She also predicted that people will live longer than 100 years in 2046 due to organ transplant technology. She also said that Earth's orbit will change in 2023, astronauts will travel to Venus in 2028, Muslims will rule Europe in 2043, and the world will end in 5079.

Many of Baba Vanga's predictions were related to politics. For example, she predicted that the 44th president of the United States would be a black man. Moreover, she seems to have predicted the development of the so-called culture war and the emergence of Donald Trump as Obama's successor at a time of cultural turmoil. According to Baba Vanga, **'Everyone hopes that he (Trump) will end it, but the opposite will happen. It will bring down the country, and the conflicts between the northern and southern states will intensify.'**

Baba Vanga correctly predicted global warming in 1955 and the Boxing Day Tsunami, saying, **'A huge wave will crush a great coastline, cover people and cities and wash everything away.'**

According to Baba Vanga, Europe would cease to exist by 2016. Obviously, that's not entirely true, but the UK voted to leave the EU on June 23, 2016, causing quite a stir. In 1989, Baba Vanga said, **'Horror, horror! American brothers will fall after being attacked by steel birds. Wolves will howl in a bush and innocent blood will be shed.'** On September 11, 2001, hijacked planes by Islamic extremists attacked the World Trade Center in New York, killing thousands.

Among her extreme predictions for the future is that, by 2066, the United States will have developed a weapon called the Environmental Destroyer that can freeze anything in its path. She also said that from 2033 to 2045, the world's glaciers will melt, causing sea and ocean levels to rise. Baba Vanga said that the world will go through many ups and downs, but when aliens start communicating with humans, the balance will be restored. She predicted that, by 2130, humans will be building deep-sea settlements. In any case, global warming justifies this prediction. According to Baba Vanga, humans will receive the technologies necessary to build colonies on the seabed and in the ocean depths from extraterrestrials. And this proves that humans can make direct physical contact with extraterrestrials before 2130.

In another of her predictions, she claimed that humans could live on Mars by 2183. But these immigrants start a rebellion that eventually leads to a nuclear confrontation. Currently, many countries and private companies, such as the United States of America, the European Space Agency (Germany, France, the Netherlands, and several other countries), Japan, India, Australia, Canada, Boeing and SpaceX, are establishing bases on Mars and competing to send their scientists and engineers to Mars; that prophecy could be fulfilled in the decades to come.

However, the incident of the rebellion and the atomic bombing of Mars could take place exactly in the same year as predicted by Baba Vanga, which is, in the year 2183. If we look at this matter logically, we will see that today, due to the competition and conflict between the Western and Eastern governments, this rebellion of human immigrants living on Mars can be viewed as a war between governments. Although nuclear states cannot use their nuclear weapons on Earth due to the coexistence conditions on a common planet, this situation does not apply to a second planet like Mars. But the most exciting prophecy of Baba Vanga is for the year 2221. She predicted that, in 2221, mankind will encounter something very terrible or gain knowledge from it in search of extraterrestrial life. But do we really have to wait until 2221 to find out this horrible fact, or are there already horrible facts in the form of proven theories? With the help of the Large Hadron Collider (LHC), scientists at CERN in Switzerland have now succeeded in discovering the smallest elementary particles of matter, the Higgs boson and the quarks, through the collision of protons and ions.

In general, there are six types of quarks: up, down, charm, strange, top, and bottom. The Higgs boson, photons, gluons, and electrons are very small, elusive particles that give mass to almost all other particles and thus form the basis of the matter that makes up us and everything else we see in the universe.

According to String Theory, these elusive particles are actually energy fields in the form of vibrating strings that can simultaneously receive and transmit all of the universe's emotions, information, and science, all stored in the Akashic Reservoir or World Cloud. The transmission speed of this data is much faster than the speed of light – almost immediately. Since more than 9.999% of the volume of all materials and particles is energy, this digital data can be called energy data. It is evident that the human body is also a substance and is made up of elements, such as carbon, hydrogen, nitrogen, calcium, phosphorus, etc. These tiny quantum particles are also present in the human brain, so by utilizing this energy transmission system, humans can not only spread their ideas and thoughts throughout the universe but can also gain access to a treasure trove of highly advanced transcendental science. The same city of knowledge that has always existed and will exist in the innermost layers of the past, present, and future. In a way, we can view the world we live in as a super-intelligent, very large computer system, or matrix, in which we are trapped as human robots. In fact, all present, past, and future events of human life are predetermined by interdimensional beings who are themselves the creators of humanity. Extraterrestrial gods arrange the course of events in the form of computer programs and then send them to us from great distances in the form of electromagnetic codes. And that's what we call fate. In a way, we can view the world and the body we are imprisoned in as a matrix that compels us to continue along the path mapped out for us in the memory of the universe. And this is the very terrible knowledge prophesized by Baba Vanga that man would attain in the year 2221.

'All the world's a stage,
And all the men and women merely players;
They have their exits and their entrances, And one man in his time plays many parts, His acts being seven ages. At first, the infant, Mewling and puking in the nurse's arms. Then the whining schoolboy, with his satchel And shining morning face, creeping like snail Unwillingly to school. And then the lover, Sighing like furnace, with a woeful ballad Made to his mistress' eyebrow. Then a soldier, Full of strange oaths and bearded like the pard, Jealous in honor, sudden and quick in quarrel, Seeking the bubble reputation Even in the cannon's mouth.

And then the justice, In fair round belly with good capon lined, With eyes severe and beard of formal cut, Full of wise saws and modern instances; And so, he plays his part. The sixth age shifts Into the lean and slippered pantaloon, With spectacles on nose and pouch on side; His youthful hose, well saved, a world too wide For his shrunk shank, and his big manly voice, Turning again towards childish treble, pipes And whistles in his sound. Last scene of all, That ends this strange eventful history, Is second childishness and mere oblivion, Sans teeth, sans eyes, sans taste, sans everything.'
William Shakespeare

In fact, like a computer, the world is made up of binary codes of zeroes and ones. Baba Vanga predicted that a huge wave would cover the beaches full of people and cities and drown everything. On December 26, 2004, a 9.1-9.3 magnitude earthquake, centred off the west coast of North Sumatra, Indonesia, generated a tsunami that killed an estimated 228,000 people in 14 countries. In fact, when Baba Vanga predicted the future, the quarks in her mind received the informational codes of those future events from the cloud of information or Akashic record hidden in the quantum layers of the universe. In other words, she could use her clairvoyance to communicate with extraterrestrial beings. However, if all the knowledge in the world is hidden in the smallest layers of the universe (in the higher dimension), then this fact can be evidence of the simultaneous discoveries and inventions throughout human history. Here are some examples of simultaneous discoveries and inventions:

- In 1998, in Japan, Takaaki Kajita, together with a team of 120 American and Japanese scientists, plus Arthur B. McDonald in Canada, proved that neutrinos have mass; although they proved that in very different ways.
- Jonas Salk and Albert Bruce Sabin both invented the polio vaccine at two different points in history.
- In 1869 and 1870, Dmitri Mendeleev and Lothar Meyer published two very similar periodic tables.
- During World War II, Hans von Ohain and Frank Whittle independently invented the jet engine on different sides of the war.
- Television, like many other innovations, has multiple inventors. In 1926, four people – John Logie Baird, Philo Farnsworth, Kenjiro Takayanagi, and Charles Francis Jenkins – succeeded in inventing television almost simultaneously.
- In 1859, Charles Darwin and Alfred Russel Wallace both proposed the theory of biological evolution through natural selection.
- Coincidentally, the film projector was invented almost simultaneously in 1895 by the Skladanowski brothers in Germany and Woodville Latham in America.
- In 1902, the stratosphere was discovered just three days apart by Richard Essen of Germany and Leon Teisserence de Bort of France.
- All knowledge about the universe lies in the innermost layers of the particles. These vibrating energy fields are known as zero-point energy. Although invisible,

this infinite ocean of quantum energy exists throughout the universe and is known as the memory of the
universe while containing all the science and information of the universe.

On the other hand, the human brain is full of electrical
activity. This electrical activity creates radiation that
can be picked up by very sensitive radio receivers. Other
brains in other places have the ability to emit such waves.
Every electron that moves in our brain can pick up radio signals from the past, and this is one of the reasons
why, throughout history, people from different conti-
nents and countries could come up with similar ideas
at the same time.

But there is another factor at play in this phenomenon, and that is the intervention of extraterrestrial beings who introduce ideas into the human mind through
telepathy. Apparently, for this purpose, aliens choose
people who have high knowledge and imagination, such
as writers, physicists, chemists, etc. If this information
is provided to people by the extraterrestrial gods themselves at the right time, it will be useful and ultimately
lead to the spiritual and mental progress of mankind. But
there are other interdimensional beings whose goal is to
destroy humanity. These extraterrestrial beings, who are
known as alien demons, cause the rapid scientific progress of mankind by transmitting scientific information
ahead of time. Consequently, the mind is unable to handle this level and amount of knowledge unless it is suffi-
ciently developed. Therefore, this situation can ultimately lead to the destruction of Planet Earth and humanity.
And that's exactly the plan the rival alien demons have

in mind: to destroy humans and conquer Planet Earth. Whatever we think will have consequences.

But the result of our opinions and thoughts is destructive. When certain ideas and research fall into human hands, new and unimaginable energies are released, and techniques that defy imagination become possible. But it will eventually happen; the question is who will have access to this information first.

For scientists, freedom of knowledge and opinion is important, nothing else. The choice they have to make is a choice that belongs to scientists. They should act scientifically and not allow themselves to be influenced by others. Scientists should pay attention to the results and logical consequences of their actions. They should try to follow a wise path. Scientists have no right to make mistakes because one wrong decision can lead to a great catastrophe. There are things that should never be risked. The destruction of humanity is one of them. We know what people are doing with the weapons they currently have, but we can't even imagine what they will do with the weapons that the new physics will create for them.

If some theories are published, the science will be disrupted, and the basis of the economy will be changed. The responsibility forces physicists to choose a different path. They should give up on their academic progress. They should avoid fame in the university and turn their backs on money in the factory. They have to leave their family in the hands of fate. They should wear mad hats and lock themselves in a mental hospital. In science, we have only reached the limit of knowledge. A few trivial and comprehensible experiments and some basic relationships between incomprehensible observations are all we know so far. The rest of the powers are a mystery that belongs to the hidden understanding of mankind.

We have reached the end of our road. Humanity is still on the way. We have progressed very quickly. No one is behind us anymore. We are facing a vacuum. Our science is terrible, our discovery is dangerous, and our knowledge is deadly. For physicists, there is only one way: obedience and submission to the truth. Truth is not strengthened by us; it is destroyed. Physicists must take back their knowledge. The only chance for physicists is to get lost and remain unknown. They can only be free in a mental hospital. They only have the right to think again in a mental hospital. Their thoughts in freedom are an explosive substance. Physicists are not crazy at all, they are murderers. Whoever kills is a murderer. Physicists have killed. Today, it is the duty of every genius to remain anonymous. Murder is horrible. Scientists must commit suicide to prevent more horrible murders. Either they stay in a mental hospital or the world becomes their mental hospital.

HIGGS BOSON

Our extraterrestrial ancestors apparently predicted human access to the Higgs boson thousands of years ago. According to the Mayan calendar, on December 21, 2012, a new window of knowledge was opened to humanity and humanity entered a new stage of science and technology. In the region of Soconusco in the state of Chiapas, Mexico, there is an ancient site called Izapa.

At this archaeological site, an image of a glowing tree-shaped gate is carved into a volcanic rock known as Stela 5. The Mayans believed that a special syrup, called Itz, flows from this tree, which can open some gates to the spiritual dimension and higher worlds. What is meant here is not the physical opening of a stargate into the higher dimension, but the opening of the Third Eye and the spiritual elevation of man into the higher dimension as a result of meditation (muraqabah). Inhaling the vapour or drinking the syrup of some herbal medicines, such as marijuana (cannabis), is also effective in man's spiritual ascension to the higher dimension and establishing communication with the extraterrestrial beings to gain insight. Then, Itz syrup is actually a kind of catalyst that facilitates the ascent of the soul into the spiritual dimension.

However, with the fulfilment of the Mayan prophecy on December 21, 2012, and the discovery of the Higgs boson, or God Particle, at CERN in Switzerland, the way to travel through space-time at the speed of light was finally paved. This discovery also makes it possible to travel to a higher dimension through the creation of artificial stargates. It also allows for time travel (future and past). Planets, stars, and, in other words, the entire physical and visible world make up less than 5% of the mass of the universe. The rest of the universe is made up of dark matter and dark energy. Dark matter is made up of very small and vibrating energy fields called the Higgs boson and quarks. Dark matter, like a vast black ocean, encompasses other visible particles in the universe. When the particles of ordinary materials collide with these vibrational energy fields, their heat and vitality decrease, and they gradually gain mass. If scientists can use the knowledge gained from the discovery of the Higgs boson to remove most of the matter, there is concern that it will create a large vacuum bubble in space-time and upset the balance of the universe. There is even the possibility that proton particle collisions at the LHC at CERN in Switzerland could cause a massive nuclear explosion similar to the Big Bang or create a black hole that engulfs the entire Earth.

THE VEDA

In Hinduism, Krishna Dvaipayana, better known as Vyasa, is a central and revered sage. He classified the Vedas and is also considered the author of the Indian heroic epic *Mahabharata*. According to Hindu belief, Vyasa is an incarnation of the god Vishnu. Today, the roots of many modern sciences can be found in Vedic texts. According to the Vedas, creation began suddenly from a tiny little point – the light from which everything was formed, and that's the Big Bang Theory.

Some physicists and inventors, such as Robert Oppenheimer, Albert Einstein, and Niels Bohr, used to read Vedic texts. Robert Oppenheimer could even read Vedic texts in Sanskrit. Vedic texts date back to 1500-1200, while the origin of the story dates back to prehistoric times when gods lived on Earth. Written in Sanskrit, these religious scriptures are the oldest sacred texts in Hinduism and have been passed down orally from generation to generation.

According to scholars, this knowledge is considered so old that it has sometimes been assumed to have existed in a time without beginning or in a distant and unknown age. That is, at the beginning of every creation. Almost all Vedic hymns are written in praise of the gods. They worship a variety of deities, some of which represent abstract qualities, such as death (Kali); beauty and devotion (Sita); friendship and harmony (Mitra); wealth and happiness (Lakshmi); kingship (Indra), language (Vacha);

wisdom (Hanuman); the natural and cosmic phenomena, like wind and storm (Rudras); fire (Agni); sun (Surya and Savitri); the forests and animals (Aranyani); Wind (Vayu); destruction (Shakti); Earth (Prithvi); Oceans (Varuna); and Dawn (Ushas).

THE TOUCH OF MEDUSA

The visible world is only 5% of the mass of the universe, and the remaining 95% is a combination of dark energy and dark matter. Even more than 99% of the volume of atoms consists of vibrating energy fields. Therefore, more than 99% of the entire universe is made up of these vibrating energy fields, called quarks. Not only is this theory confirmed by string theory, but the existence of these smallest quantum particles was proven by the discovery of the Higgs boson at CERN in Switzerland in 2012. In fact, the entire observable physical world, including stars, planets, and other space objects, as well as dark matter and dark energy, are all connected through these infinite micro-energy fields in the boundless ocean of the universe.

All information and energies in the universe can be transmitted almost instantaneously from one point to the farthest ends of the universe. The human mind is also a part of the universe, so our mind radiates energy just like other parts and phenomena of this world. However, according to the Yin & Yang philosophy that everything has its opposite, energy also has two opposite types, positive and negative. When we cultivate positive thoughts in our mind, positive energies are unintentionally transferred to our environment, but when we think of negative issues, we create negative ripples in the environment.

Negative thoughts allow evil forces to gain strength. War, violence, rape, and murder are all rooted in the negative waves that flow through the air. There are people who create disaster just by looking at people and things. This phenomenon is called the Devil's Gaze, or the Medusa Touch, which is always destructive.

Medusa was the daughter of Phorcys and Setu, one of the ancient gods of the sea in Greek mythology. He was born on the island of Sarpedon and was one of the three monstrous gorgons. However, unlike his brothers and sisters, he was mortal and therefore vulnerable to the laws of nature and the whims of the gods.

Medusa was originally a very sexy girl with gorgeous hair, but this beauty eventually led to her misfortune. She slept with Poseidon, the god of the sea, in Athena's temple, thus defiling Athena's temple. To punish her, Athena transformed her into the ugliest and most hated creature that ever existed, the Gorgon, a monster with sharp fangs and hair made of living, venomous snakes and a hideous face that would terrify anyone who came across it. If it looked at someone, it would instantly turn that person into stone. There were three Gorgons in total, Euryale, Stheno, and Medusa. Traditionally, two of the Gorgons, Stheno and Euryale, were immortal, but their sister, Medusa, was not. Perseus was the son of Zeus and Danae and had promised Polydectes to bring him Medusa's head. Perseus had help from both gods and nymphs. The latter gave him several magical items to aid him in his quest: winged sandals that enabled him to fly, a shoulder bag, and the helmet of Hades. This last magical device was very useful as it made anyone wearing it invisible. With these weapons and protective equipment, Perseus went in search of Medusa, one of the three Gorgons.

Perseus found Medusa's cave with the gifts of the gods and entered it. Perseus found Medusa sleeping in her cave and was careful not to wake her. Perseus took Athena's reflective bronze shield and held it up to use as a mirror to find Medusa. As he moved towards Medusa, Perseus held up the shield so he could have a clear view of Medusa, making sure he was only looking at Medusa on the shield.

When Perseus approached Medusa, he took the sword that Hephaestus had given him and severed the monster's head. At this time, two mythical creatures, Pegasus, the immortal winged horse, and Chrysaor, both sons of Medusa and Poseidon, emerged from Medusa's neck. On his return, Perseus gave Athena the head of Medusa, and she placed it on Zeus' shield on her breast. Today, this sign can be seen in the statues of Athena.

Telekinesis is a hypothetical psychic ability that allows a person to affect a physical system without physical interaction. In other words, it is the power of the mind on objects. There is a girl who can move the chair around the room with her mind. Traditionally, the power of thought was used to endure pain. There are people who are able to put pointed sticks in their bodies or sleep on pointed sticks and can walk through fire without feeling any pain or getting wounds or burns on their bodies.

In America in 1974, a boy named Kevin could use his mind to turn on the lights on the scoreboard and ring the bell. Nina Kulagina was a Leningrad housewife who could move objects without touching them. Forty senior scientists searched her for magnets, wires and artificial devices, but nothing was found. They could find no reason for her ability to move objects. In 1970, a young history teacher named Jorgensen in Denmark was able to break a glass frame from a few metres away with the power of his mind.

Disasters are endless. Tornadoes, floods, earthquakes, plane crashes, space shuttle explosions, tsunamis, coronas, the Chernobyl disaster, famine, drought, volcanic eruptions, and shipwrecks.

It makes one wonder: How many of these children of Satan who have the power to create disaster are really among us humans?

THE WEAPONS OF THE GODS

In the Indus Valley, the ruins of a very old and advanced civilization called Rama have attracted the attention of archaeologists for decades. This roughly 15,000-year-old civilization coincided with the Atlantean civilization, ruled by very wise and learned kings who were also priests.

Rama's civilization consisted of seven great cities, which are called the Seven Rishis in Sanskrit texts. The ruins of one of these cities is located in north-western India, called Harappa, and there are other ruins in eastern Pakistan, called Mohenjo-daro. Mohenjo-daro and Harappa are unusual because of their advanced civilization and technology. It is clear that these two cities were built based on detailed architectural plans. Also, their very modern sewage system is much more advanced than the sewage system that exists in these areas today.

In the city of Mohenjo-daro, there is a great bath that was filled by the Indus. It was probably a public bath and a large social area used for special religious ceremonies. It is estimated that around 40,000 people lived in Mohenjo-daro. These people played parlour games, like chess, traded in gems and precious stones, and cared about cleanliness and hygiene. Parallel to the Rama civilization in the east, there was another highly developed civilization in the west, called Atlantis, located in the middle of the Atlantic Ocean. These two civilizations were constantly at war with each other. Both civilizations were equipped with sophisticated weaponry and aircraft never seen before. One of these aircraft was called Vimana.

In ancient India, these flying chariots were used by the gods for transportation and battle. According to the Vedic scriptures, these flying chariots came in various sizes and shapes. There was the Elephant Vimana with multiple engines, the Agnihotra Vimana with two engines, and so on. They could travel at different speeds to different heights and distances. In Hindu texts and Sanskrit epics, Vimanas are described as circular planes over two decks with portholes and a dome. However, another group of Vimanas are described in the form of cigarettes or cylinders, capable of locomotion both in air and underwater. These Vimanas could fly at flying wind speed and produce a melodious sound during flight. Some of these Vimanas were short-haul aircraft, while others were built for long-distance and intercontinental travel. However, there was another type that the gods used for outer space and interplanetary travel. These ancient space shuttles were indestructible and used special technology that allowed them to become invisible to enemy space shuttles. In addition, they were equipped with another type of technology that allowed them to disable all electrical systems of enemy space shuttles and put them into a state of suspended animation, thereby seriously damaging them. According to *Mahabharata* and *Ramayana*, vimanas were kept in a Vimana Griha, a kind of hangar. They are said to be produced by mercury or a yellowish-white viscous liquid, like gasoline. Sanskrit texts say that when the Vimanas were in motion, they shot a roaring flame from behind, reminiscent of modern jet engines.

In ancient Indian texts and paintings, the god Vishnu is usually seen flying on his Garuda. Garuda was famous for throwing bombs, flying to the moon, and taking Vishnu to different parts of the solar system. During World War II, the Nazis regularly sent delegations to the East to gain access to the secret knowledge and technology of the ancient Hindus. Sanskrit texts are believed to have been the source of many ideas for Nazi scientists in many of their inventions, including the jet-propulsion engine (V1 and V2) and Die Glocke. Indian pyramids are built as if Vimana is sitting on them. Vimana is described in the *Mahabharata* as follows:

'Vimana was very advanced and equipped. Neither the gods nor the demons had the ability to overcome it. Vimana was like a cloud during the day while it roared like thunder in the night sky. Its beauty captivated the minds of all who saw it. Viswakarma, the master of design and construction, had created it with his unique skill, though its outline, like that of the sun, was not easily described.'

According to ancient Sanskrit texts, the Atlanteans had their own flying machines called the Vailixi. These space shuttles were cylindrical in shape and could move both underwater and in space. Another weapon mentioned in *Mahabharata* is Vajra. This weapon belonged to Indra, who was known in ancient India as the god of storms and wars. Indra's arrow (Vajra) was propelled by a circular reflector. When ignited, it would produce a beam of light that would instantly turn it to ash if it hit a target. Sanskrit scriptures, such as the *Ramayana* and the *Mahabharata*, tell the story of a terrible battle between the Ramas and the Atlanteans that took place some 12,000 years ago, in which weapons of mass destruction were used.

'Gurkha, flying a swift and
powerful Vimana (fast aircraft)
hurled a single projectile (rocket)
charged with the power
of the Universe (nuclear device).
An incandescent column of
smoke and flame, as bright as
ten thousand suns, rose with
all its splendour.
It was an unknown weapon,
an iron thunderbolt, a gigantic
messenger of death,
which reduced to ashes the entire race
of the Vrishnis and the Andhakas.
The corpses were so burned
as to be unrecognizable.
Hair and nails fell out;
Pottery broke without apparent cause,
and the birds turned white.
... After a few hours all foodstuffs were infected ...
... to escape from this fire the soldiers threw
themselves in streams to wash
themselves and their equipment.'
Mahabharata

Here the *Mahabharata* seems to be describing a nuclear war. After excavating Mohenjo-daro, archaeologists found skeletons lying in the streets, some of which were seen hand in hand as if they had been destroyed together by some freak disaster. To their surprise, scientists found that the intensity of radioactivity in these skeletons was much higher than normal. The brick and stone walls were glazed. Stone and brick usually vitrify (turn into glass) when exposed to extreme heat. The streets were covered with pieces of black glass. It was discovered that these lumps of glass were clay pots that had melted at high heat!

In addition, before the site was excavated, a layer of radioactive ash was found in the ground, confirming the theory of a nuclear event that could have destroyed the ancient city. Both the Rama and the Atlanteans used weapons of mass destruction. The battlefields were not only on Earth but also on the moon. Eventually, Atlantis destroyed the Rama Empire with a terrible weapon (the atomic bomb). Hundreds of years after the annihilation of the Rama civilization, the Atlanteans became greedy, arrogant, and morally bankrupt. Therefore, as a result of their disobedience, they gradually lost their popularity with the gods.

As punishment, the gods sent fire and earthquakes and sank Atlantis into the sea. After the destruction of the Rama civilization by nuclear weapons and the catastrophic sinking of Atlantis, the world collapsed into the Stone Age, while the first civilizations appeared thousands of years later in Mesopotamia and Egypt.

NIKOLA TESLA

Nikola Tesla was born on July 10, 1856, in the village of Smiljan, which lies on the border of modern-day Croatia, which was then part of the Austrian Empire. He was one of the most influential figures of the 19th century, but his name is always overshadowed by Edison. He not only revolutionized the research of scientists before him but also took a huge step in the development of science, surpassing the scientists of his time. In 1884, Tesla visited Thomas Edison in America to fulfil his dreams. He was initially responsible for modifying Edison's DC design under his supervision. After a while, Tesla proposed the idea of alternating current to Edison, but he was met with strong opposition. As a result, he began his practical activity independently with the support of some capitalists of his time. After some time, however, his AC idea was able to beat Edison's DC idea. Until the 20th century, electricity was just a scientific curiosity and many people doubted its effectiveness.

The success of Tesla's plan was not only a turning point in the world, but also led him to fulfil his childhood dream of generating electricity at Niagara Falls. On November 16, 1896, lights began to turn on in parts of New York City, and soon all of New York was electrified. Tesla's research on electricity was only part of the innovations that made him famous. However, he patented more than 278 inventions during his lifetime. Tesla claimed that he was in contact with extraterrestrial beings, and, in fact, they dictated to him the design and information necessary for his inventions. Tesla experienced sparks of light that gave him moments of creativity and enlightenment. He believed that we humans are receivers, and all ideas come to us from other worlds. Tesla was able to dissect all of these inventions piece by piece in his head and he knew exactly how to make these inventions based on his own mental experiences.

In 1915, Tesla decided to create a powerful weapon that would help its owner win in any battle. He worked on this plan for many years before finally announcing in 1934 that he had succeeded in creating such a weapon. Explaining his weapon, Tesla said that it could prevent war in the world forever, comparing it to something like the Great Wall of China, which could protect the borders of countries. Newspapers called Tesla's weapon the Death Ray or the Peace Ray, but Tesla called his new invention 'the Teleforce'. Tesla had come to the conclusion that it would be better to use charged particles in the design of his weapon. According to Tesla's own manuscripts, such particles can travel at 84 times the speed of sound. Tesla decided to build the Teleforce as high as Wardenclyffe Tower to destroy anything that got too close. At the very beginning, Tesla wrote a letter to JP Morgan Jr. and asked him to invest in his new project, but Morgan did not take his words seriously. In 1937, Tesla wrote an article in which he tried to simply explain the workings and design of his gun. Tesla's description is very similar to what is known today as high-energy particle beam weapons. Tesla invited several different countries, including the United Kingdom and the United States, to invest in the Teleforce project, but no country accepted. However, some say that the Soviet government agreed to Tesla's request and paid him $25,000, but Tesla never managed to deliver anything to them. Certainly, the failure of the Wardenclyffe Tower left a bad memory in people's minds, and investors weren't ready to invest in another Tesla project so easily. It's not clear if Tesla built a prototype or not. Some say Teleforce didn't work at all. Toward the end of his life, Tesla claimed that some people searched his hotel room to steal secrets of the Teleforce, but found nothing. Tesla said he didn't put most of his research on Teleforce on paper and kept it all in his head. However, some say that Teleforce actually worked and Tesla wrote his research on paper, but the FBI stole his manuscripts when they searched his room after his death. They believe that many of the current weapons were made from these manuscripts.

But, so far, no one has been able to prove anything. In fact, we are all thieves. Only fraudsters deny it. In fact, man is a creature that imitates nature. This theory is confirmed by the great Greek philosopher Socrates, who says that art is an imitation of nature. Today, it is proven that the origin of many human inventions and discoveries can be found in ancient texts, such as the Vedas, Mahabharata, Ramayana, The Diary of Merer (Papyrus Jarf), and the ancient Mesopotamian clay tablets, such as the Seven Tablets of Creation, the Dead Sea Scrolls.

However, these documents are only written records of oral stories that have been passed down from generation to generation since prehistoric times, when our extraterrestrial gods lived on Earth at the same time as humans – extraterrestrial gods who themselves follow the universe and its governing laws.

Tesla built the Wardenclyffe Tower in New York in 1901-1902 with the investment of JP Morgan. Tesla's design was the world's prototype for wireless communications. At first, Morgan thought Tesla's goal in building this tower was to transmit power and information around the world, and he invested $150,000 to do so. Tesla explained his plan as follows: **'If wireless communication is adopted and implemented worldwide, the earth will become like a big brain that can react at any time and from any point in the world.'** However, he had a more ambitious goal than wireless communication. He planned to use the conductivity of the Earth's crust to achieve a free and unlimited source of energy. Tesla believed that Earth's inhabitants could get free electricity by sinking an iron rod into the ground. If this idea were to come true, the situation of energy supply on Earth would change completely. But after Morgan stopped funding the project, Tesla also abandoned the project. Tesla has patented hundreds of inventions during his incredibly productive life, including:

1. Tesla coil that could transmit electricity wirelessly.
2. Tesla turbine
3. Radio
4. Tesla magnifying glass
5. Tesla alternating current
6. Tesla induction motor
7. Tesla hydroelectric power
8. Tesla neon lamps
9. Tesla valve

In 1897, a radio patent was filed in Tesla's name, but, in 1904, Marconi, who had good connections with Edison and Andre Carneggio (one of the Patent Office employees), took the patent from Tesla and filed it in his name. Tesla fought hard but couldn't get any results. Finally, in 1943, the U.S. Supreme Court took Marconi's patent away and gave it to Tesla.

In 1911, Nikola Tesla had an interview with the *New York Herald* newspaper and made a strange claim. In this interview, he said that he is building a car called the Flying Saucer! He continued, **'The thing I'm going to invent isn't at all like today's flying objects, which means you won't see wings or grasshoppers in it. In fact, this is an anti-gravity machine and can move at very high speeds. It offers absolute safety and can keep its resilience for a long time and stand stable in the sky even in a violent storm!'** The fact that this plane used free energy as fuel was an advantage for it. And maybe that's why no country was willing to invest in it, considering that the aerospace and automotive industries were completely dependent on oil at the time.

In 1893, Tesla patented a mechanical vibrator that ran on steam and could use its vibrations to generate electricity. As Tesla later told reporters, while he was calibrating the machine for an experiment, the machine shook his New York City lab so severely that it nearly destroyed the entire building. He said, **'Suddenly, all the heavy machinery was flying through the lab. I took a hammer and broke this device. If it had continued working in a few minutes, the building would have collapsed above us. Everyone gathered in front of the building on the street, and then the police and ambulance came. I told my assistants not to say anything. We told the police it must have been an earthquake.**

That's all they know about the incident.' This mysterious device inspired Tesla to build a geodynamic televibrator, which was actually an earthquake machine that could help scientists discover the Earth's geological features, as well as help engineers and researchers, discover underground mineral deposits and find metals.

VRIL-GESELLSCHAFT

Scientific advances are all about the visible world, but certainly not enough to travel to the higher dimension. This cannot be achieved even by creating a small stargate. But even to achieve these mundane technologies, humans are powerless without help and communication with extraterrestrials.

During the Second World War, the Nazi military worked on the creation of UFOs, and there are even undeniable documents about their success and progress in this field. The goal of the Nazis in those years was to become a superpower and dominate the world. To achieve this goal, they kept trying to build a powerful army and equip it with advanced weapons and technologies. Therefore, they were forced to investigate secret cults, mystical powers, legends, secret organizations, the Ark of the Covenant, and many forgotten ancient teachings at the behest of the leader of the Nazi Party, Adolf Hitler. For this, they formed special teams, and one of these organizations was the Vril secret society. At the same time, Vril is the name of an infinite and mysterious source of energy from which the gods derive their power.

According to occult and ancient teachings, **'everything is spirit.'** The world is mental. If you can harness this life force, you will reach a point where magic meets reality, where power dances at your fingertips, and where God meets man. With the energy of Vril, you will harness the life force of the gods, great wonders, and mysteries. By learning to use your mind correctly and magically, you will be able to create change and make your life magical. It is actually the magical power of your mind that allows you to manipulate Vril energy.

The Vril is still a power unknown to mankind. Only through meditation, reading a series of verses, and performing a series of specific actions can you control your mind over time and gain access to this power.

Vril can be considered a form of energy, like electricity, that can be converted by an engineer into different energies, like heat, light, or sound. But the difference is that Vril's energy can be converted into any other type of energy. The Vril Society also believed that they could use this energy to power the Nazi army's war machines and weapons. They also planned to use this energy in aeroplanes and flying saucers.

The idea of Vril was first mentioned by Edward Bulwer Lytton in his novel, *The Power of the Coming Race*. In this book, Lytton mentions an ancient underground civilization called the Vril Society (Vril-ya). This noble race had managed to acquire the eternal energy of Viral. And whoever possessed this source of energy could be the ruler of the entire universe and all the planets in it. Lytton emphasizes that all human activity and effort should be focused on finding and discovering this source of energy. Willy Ley, a big name in the rocket industry, published an article titled Pseudoscience in Naziland in 1933 after fleeing Germany. This article mentions the name of Vril as both a secret society and as a source of energy used by the Nazis to manufacture UFOs. At the beginning of World War II, the Nazis founded the Vril Society on Hitler's orders to make new discoveries and further their war aims.

The purpose of founding the Vril Society was to gain the ability to control the human mind, create supernatural weapons of mass destruction, and experiment with paranormal science under the leadership of Adolf Hitler in Berlin. It can be said with certainty that this group played a significant role in the discovery, invention, and development of many modern weapons and technologies.

After the defeat of the Nazis, all these documents fell into the hands of the countries that conquered Berlin. Today, all these countries are among the most advanced and powerful countries in the world. It is said that, after the defeat of the Nazis, the Vril Society withdrew to a base in Antarctica and disappeared into the hollow Earth to meet with the leaders of an advanced race inhabiting the inner Earth. During the Nazi era, science, technology, and industry experienced a breathtaking acceleration and advancement because Hitler wanted all of Germany's industries to focus on war-related inventions and discoveries. And this led to significant advances in science in the field of industry, technology, and medicine in those years. There are many documents about the great inventions and advanced technologies of the Nazis during World War II.

The UFOs, night vision systems, and jet engine technology were all first invented by the Nazis during World War II. These technologies were so advanced at the time that many believed Adolf Hitler could only obtain these technologies with the help of extraterrestrials. If you look at the progress and development of aviation technology over the course of history, you can see that aeroplanes were initially built with three wings, later with two wings, and, during the Nazi era, with single wings.

During the Second World War, these aircraft were further developed and, contrary to the usual procedure, achieved rapid development by being equipped with jet engines. These aircraft flew two to three times faster than their predecessors, so anti-aircraft systems could not intercept them. When these planes appeared on the battlefield, all the soldiers on the other side were scared. V-1 rockets were among the achievements of the Vril Society, developed and used by Nazi engineers during World War II. These missiles were also called flying bombs. These missiles flew in the form of small drones and can be considered the prototype of today's cruise missiles. About 30,000 V-1 rockets were produced at that time. About 10,000 of these rockets were fired at England, and at least 2,419 of them hit London alone. They inflicted terrible casualties and created eight stressful and nightmarish months for the British people and the British Army.

The technology of this rocket belonged to a German scientist named Werner von Braun, who was a member of the Saal-Schutz (SS). Then, Von Braun joined NASA after World War II and was the designer of the first rocket launched to the Moon. In the Vril project, the V-2 was the first synthetic ballistic missile capable of exiting Earth's atmosphere, and it can be considered the prototype of today's modern missiles and the first missiles sent to the Moon. Adolf Hitler's insatiable greed led to him wanting more. In fact, in order to gain more power, after Hitler founded the Vril Society, he pressured the members of this organization to give him the technologies of extraterrestrial beings. He claimed they had developed some technologies superior to the V-2 project.

According to the surviving documents, at the end of the war, the Vril Society was working on a rocket, called New York, and as the name suggests, their goal in building this rocket was to strike this city in the United States of America. It also became clear that Berlin had gone much further and started researching rockets that could reach Mars. However, the German scientists were also held in high esteem by their enemies. But where did all this technology really come from? Were the Nazis smarter than their counterparts in other countries, or did they spend more money on their research? Or, according to supernatural theories and ideas, maybe the ancient supernatural sciences and extraterrestrial powers were really involved?

Nazi scholars regularly studied ancient Sanskrit texts, such as the Bhagavad Gita, Mahabharata, and Ramayana. Flying chariots (Vimanas) are frequently mentioned in these texts. The Pushpaka Vimana, as mentioned in the mythological scripture Ramayana, was King Ravana's flying chariot. In the Ramayana, it is mentioned that the Pushpaka Vimana resembled the sun and could go anywhere at will. According to the Ramayana, the Pushpaka Vimana was originally built by Vishwakarma for Brahma, the Hindu god of creation. Brahma later gave it to Cobra, the god of wealth, then it was stolen by his half-brother, King Ravana, along with Lanka. It is believed that Nazi scientists unravelled the secret of the construction and technology of these very advanced ancient UFOs by studying these ancient Indian epic texts. As mentioned in the Vedas, these flying vimanas used some kind of Mercury propulsion system that allowed them to defy gravity and stay aloft. In 1936, three years before the start of the Second World War, a flying object crashed in the Black Forest near Freiburg. Shortly thereafter, the Nazis quarantined the area and found a disc-shaped plane with some strange creatures inside. It was said that these grey creatures resembled mole crickets. They were described as creatures with big heads and eyes and small bodies, very similar to the aliens in the Roswell, New Mexico, incident. Then, they took these grey creatures to a nearby secret Nazi military base for further investigation. Heinrich Himmler is said to have secretly gone to that military base a few days later and chained himself there. No one knows what Himmler was doing in that secret military base that night. According to the guards, in the middle of the night, they heard Himmler screaming from the hall where he had chained himself.

After the Black Forest event, scientists began researching antigravity. One of these researchers was the Austrian scientist Viktor Schauberger, who had done much research on vortex science and nature. This scientist, who was captured by the Nazis, was nicknamed the Water Witch. He spent his whole childhood in the forests of Austria, and his only dream and goal was to become a pasture engineer. But before that day came true, he managed to discover the magic of water. By using the repulsive properties of water and the knowledge of vortex science, as well as by inventing air turbines, Schauberger succeeded in constructing systems with which the greatest possible energy could be extracted from the weather.

According to scientists, the source of the Vril energy was not based on electricity, but they believed in the existence of energy in nature. Schauberger's view of this experiment was based on animals. And the question that occupied him was: How can animals float in air and water? How is it possible for a fish to stay in a raging river without moving an inch? Does the fish swim in the water or does the water make the fish swim? According to Schauberger, a fish does not swim, but the water makes it swim. The bird does not fly; it is propelled by the warm air current. All of today's vehicles, including automobiles, aeroplanes, and ships, are also powered by motive power. But Viktor Schauberger wanted to implement this idea in cars. He wanted to move the air in a special way so that the car wasn't pushed forwards but pulled forwards. In 1953, he sent a letter to one of his closest friends. In part of his letter, he wrote that the maximum energy extracted from water can be so high that it would make no sense to use nuclear energy instead. Schauberger was able to invent a device that created a vortex. In other words, it was an artificial storm generator. The invention of this device made him known as the inventor of the UFO. This idea was considered a revolutionary idea in those years.

According to Schauberger's studies of the Sanskrit scriptures, thousands of years ago in India, there was a flying machine called Vimana that used some sort of anti-gravity technology to fly. The Vril organization attempted to translate these writings into German, and as a result, by summarizing this information, they began to build their own UFOs. By developing air turbines, Schauberger was able to increase airflow to its maximum power, and, by using wave-generating disks, he was able to balance the maximum flow of energy with transmission channels, thus designing the first artificial UFO. Finally, in 1939, after three years, the Nazis managed to build a UFO-like aircraft using their knowledge of the

Black Forest incident and the Sanskrit scriptures. The first UFOs built by the Nazis were 20 metres (65.5 feet) high and could carry eight people.

During World War II, Nazi scientists invented a bell-shaped device that was 3.5 metres (11.5 feet) high and 2.7 metres (about 9 feet) in diameter for time travel. They called this time machine Die Glocke. In 2000, a Polish writer and journalist, named Igor Witkowski, first published material about Die Glocke. Witkowski claimed to have learned of the device through contact with the Polish Secret Service. He also claimed that, during one of his interrogations, an SS officer talked about Die Glocke and mysterious Nazi experiments. Witkowski, who had access to interrogation reports, claimed that the Nazis conducted strange experiments near the Czech border during the war. After this information was released, other authors, such as Nick Cook and Joseph P. Farrell, had sparked various debates about the Bell's connection to antigravity systems and even time travel devices.

Debates about the connection between Nazi developments and paranormal science have always been heated. Cases like this bell-like object have fuelled such debates and made conspiracy theories about secret UFO companies, aliens, and other science fiction ideas even more controversial. German scientists are said to have made Die Glocke from a series of very hard and heavy alloys under the supervision of SS officers. According to Cook's interview with Witkowski, Die Glocke consisted of two rotating cylinders filled with a liquid metal similar to mercury. This liquid was called Xerum 525 and was kept by scientists in a lead container with a height of one metre (3.25 feet).

Witkowski said other metals, such as Thorium and Beryllium were also used in the device's construction, and since building an anti-gravity engine was the main goal of Die Glocke project, Nazi technicians chained it to concrete pillars as it swung back and forth through the air during testing. In addition, Witkowski noted in his book that when the bell was turned on, living beings within 200 metres (656 feet) would experience terrifying effects, such as blood clots, the disintegration of body tissues, headaches, and delirium. According to Witkowski's documents, near the village of Lodwicz Kłodzkie in Silesia, Poland, there is a concrete structure called The Henge, which appears to have been the site of Die Glocke testing.

The Die Glock project was one of the most famous scientific and military Nazi projects. During World War II, the Nazis spent a lot of money and time on this project, so this project made the Nazis less worried about making the atomic bomb. But, on the other side of the war, the Americans made the first atomic bomb and won the war. Dr Joseph Farrell wrote in his book, *Roswell and Reich*, that some kind of stargate technology was used in Die Glocke. This technology is actually a type of web-based technology related to supernatural dimensions, and Nazi scientists have tried to investigate its possible applications in three areas:

1. Zero-point energy (the lowest possible energy that a quantum mechanical system can have)
2. Gravity (the invisible force that pulls objects towards each other) and its manipulation
3. Development of a very dangerous weapon

Today, we know that the phenomenon of time travel is theoretically possible, and the famous German physicist Albert Einstein proved this theory in his theory of general relativity. By the time the Allies invaded Germany, the entire project of Die Glocke and its commander, Hans Kammler, had already been destroyed, and no trace of them could be found. On December 9, 1965, residents of Cooksburg, Pennsylvania, in the U.S., saw a fireball moving across the dark evening sky before landing. This huge oak-shaped object looked like Die Glocke, the Nazi time travel machine. Was that flying object really the Nazi Bell? If yes, what happened to Hans Kemmler? The area where the object fell was immediately cordoned off by local authorities until U.S. Army engineers and scientists arrived to inspect the site. Government officials have ruled out possible theories, such as a plane crash, a failed rocket test or remains of space satellites entering the atmosphere. They said the fireball was probably a meteor entering Earth's atmosphere. If we look at all the technologies we have today, we will see that they are all derived from the same technologies invented and used by German scientists during World War II.

After World War II, there were not two separate American and Russian missile development programs in the world, but only one German missile development program, which both the Americans and the Russians began to develop with the help of thousands of German scientists. After the end of World War II, the Americans arrested thousands of Nazi scientists and brought them to America during an operation called Paper Clip. The Americans cleared all the previous Nazi backgrounds of these scientists and engineers and gave them American citizenship so that they could bring their rich knowledge to the technological development of America. One of those scientists was Wernher von Braun, who was a member of the NSDAP and a leading figure in the development of Nazi rocket technology and one of the pioneers of rocket and space technology in the United States. Von Braun is best known today as director of the NASA engineering program, chief architect of the Apollo V-2 rocket and development of the Saturn V rocket. Another of those German scientists was Robert Oppenheimer, who is known as the father of the atomic bomb. Oppenheimer was one of the observers at the Trinity test in New Mexico, where the first atomic bomb was successfully detonated on July 16, 1945. He later said that after the atomic explosion, a passage from the famous Hindu scripture Bhagavad Gita came to his mind: **'Now I become death, destroyer of worlds.'**

Oppenheimer describes the moments after the atomic explosion as follows:

'We waited until the explosion was over, got out of the bunker, and then things got really serious. We knew the world would never be the same again. A few people laughed. A few people cried. Most people were silent.'

In August 1945, American bombers dropped atomic bombs on Hiroshima and Nagasaki in Japan. This was the first time that nuclear weapons were used in war. The bomb killed 80,000 people instantly, and tens of thousands later died from exposure to that nuclear radiation.

Another great and prominent Nazi scientist, who is considered one of the great pioneers and theoreticians of the history of the space age, was Hermann Oberth. In his youth, he published his research in the form of several books, and, during World War II, he worked continuously at the Nazi rocket research centre. In 1955, Oberth moved to the United States to once again work with von Braun, this time on the development of space-capable rockets for the U.S. military. Their collaboration led to the development of the Saturn V rocket that carried humans to the moon. Hermann Oberth first announced, during World War II, that ballistic missiles could have the ability to leave Earth and fly into space. But, at that time, this topic was not considered very important for the Nazis. The Nazis only wanted to attack distant countries with ballistic missiles. Oberth has written books on future space developments and also believed in extraterrestrial theories. From this, it can be concluded that the American space agency (NASA) owes many of its space and rocket successes to German scientists.

NAZI SWASTIKA

The swastika, used as a symbol of Nazi persecution during World War II, is 3,000 years old. The swastika means happiness or well-being in the ancient Indian language of Sanskrit. The strange thing is that this symbol can be seen in every corner of the world. In India, in Iran, in Egypt, and in all countries with ancient civilizations. Were the Nazis aware of this symbol's association with extraterrestrial beings?

According to the Sanskrit scriptures, the swastika symbol was associated with extraterrestrial beings such as Lord Brahma, known as the god of creation in the Hindu religion. This god along with Vishnu and Shiva formed a triune god named Trimurti. Brahma is the creator god, Shiva is the destroyer god, and Vishnu is the protector god. Unlike humans and other animals that live in the physical world, who are usually male and female, the gods that belong to the spiritual world are neither male nor female in terms of gender. In fact, they are neutral. When the immortal spirits of extraterrestrial gods enter the visible and physical world in which we humans live, they can take any form and gender. For example, they can take the form of animals such as cows, elephants, lions, falcons, and even a combination of these. The rival extraterrestrial beings that come to our physical world from the higher dimension – and we know them as devils – like our extraterrestrial gods, are gender neutral, that is, they are neither male nor female.

This extraterrestrial technology (transition from the spiritual state to different physical bodies and vice versa) is the reason why exorcists often describe the appearance of demonic beings as a combination of multiple beings such as elephants, snakes, humans, etc. In fact, the extraterrestrial demons trick people into committing crimes by entering the spiritual phase and capturing their bodies. However, demons only prey on people who, by having hateful thoughts, send negative energies around and cultivate negative thoughts in their minds. Basically, demons don't waste their time and energy trying to seduce good people because it has no effect on them.

Brahma is used by Hindus as a symbol of extraterrestrial beings in religious ceremonies. Brahma is one of the most important gods of Hinduism. Brahma is omnipotent and the creator of the universe. According to the Brahmin belief, on the first day of creation, this god created priests from his mouth, warriors from his chest, workers from his thighs, and the dead from his feet. In fact, he is the supreme creator of the universe. People who worship Brahma believe that he is embodied in human form with four arms holding a dish, a rosary, a sacred spoon and a copy of the Vedas.

Another main deity of Hinduism is Shiva, who is also known as the god of destruction and anger. Lord Shiva is usually depicted as a woman or a man sitting on a tiger skin and carrying a snake on his shoulder. Another important characteristic of Shiva is that he has a third eye on his forehead and wears earrings in his ears. Next to him, there is usually a container with the water of life. As one of the most complex deities of India, Shiva has seemingly contradictory characteristics. He is the destroyer and the restorer, the great ascetic and the embodiment of sensuality, the benevolent shepherd, and the vengeful warrior. His weapons are snake, leopard, spear, earthquake, flood, and war. One of Shiva's weapons is a secret weapon known as the Dance of Death, and, indeed, when Shiva dances, it brings destruction. According to Hinduism, evil and destruction in the world should coexist with good to keep the balance. For this reason, Shiva, although he is the god of destruction, is considered a holy god among the Hindus, and they worship him.

In Hinduism, Vishnu is the presiding deity within the Trimurti and is considered the guardian of the universe. His duty is to return to Earth in turbulent times and restore the balance between good and evil. He has four arms, the two arms in front symbolizing his presence in the human world and the two arms behind him representing his relationship with the spiritual realm. In many images, his hands hold his four important symbols: the conch shell, the chakra or disc, the mace, and the lotus flower. Vishnu is usually depicted reclining on a large coiled serpent or riding a human-shaped scorpion with an eagle's head. Hinduism teaches that, when mankind is threatened by evil forces, Vishnu descends to restore justice and help mankind. In Hinduism, Vishnu is said to have come to Earth in several incarnations to restore the balance between good and evil in the world. The incarnations that Vishnu takes are called avatars. Hindus believe that Buddha was the embodiment of Vishnu on Earth. The phenomenon of the incarnation of alien gods in the bodies of certain people has occurred many times throughout history and for certain purposes, for example, to guide people morally and lead them on an honourable path.

In Christianity, belief in the divinity of Jesus Christ can be justified in the same way. When Christians refer to the Trinity (Father, Son, and Holy Spirit), they are actually referring to an extraterrestrial Spirit (the Holy Spirit), who incarnated in a physical body (God, the Son) 2,023 years ago. In fact, the Holy Spirit and God, the Son, form a common entity called God, the Father.

Apparently, the swastika had magical powers bestowed upon the ancient Indians by aliens. The Nazis were interested in ancient epics and mystery cults. They constantly studied ancient writings to discover the scientific secrets hidden in them. Therefore, the Nazis spent a lot of money, time, and energy to obtain this information. They constantly sent expeditions around the world to gather information and knowledge that could help them win the war. Heinrich Himmler, who can be seen as Hitler's right-hand man and at the head of the Nazis and the SS, was a person who was very interested in secret and sinister cults. It is said that he had a terrifying castle where he performed evil rituals out of sight.

At his castle in Born, Westphalia, Himmler assembled a group of mediums and humans who claimed to be able to communicate with extraterrestrials. One of these people was the most important member of the Vril group, Maria Orsic. Maria was also the head of Vril's women's branch called Vrilian. This group consisted of a number of beautiful women with long hair because they believed that long hair acted as a receiving antenna of the Vril energy source. Maria held ceremonies to summon the spirits of interdimensional beings for Nazi leaders, including Hitler. At these ceremonies, she spoke to the Nazi leaders of a particular race of extraterrestrial beings known as the Star Race or Aryan Race. They believed that these creatures came to Earth through the mother star-gate, Aldebaran, located in the constellation of Taurus. Maria's job was to relay their words to the leaders of the Nazi army. After taking power in 1933, Adolf Hitler mobilized his circle of allies and the Vril cult for extensive research into extraterrestrials.

Aliens have apparently lived alongside mankind on this planet throughout human history. Even the idea of building UFOs stems from the technologies of ancient civilizations created by interdimensional beings from tens of thousands of years ago. Dr Hermann Oberth, who worked on the Nazi Army's rocket research project for the Nazi military, claimed to have received help from extraterrestrials.

As Adolf Hitler's power grew day by day, he began sending groups to the most remote parts of the world to search for the Ark of the Covenant. According to legend, the ancient Egyptians used the Ark of the Covenant in the Great Pyramid of Giza to direct electricity generated from subterranean water to the golden top of the pyramid so they could send that amount of electricity to specific locations in the city. It is said that the ancient Egyptians used some kind of electric lamp instead of primitive lighting devices, like torches or fire. The arc light used in the lighthouse of Alexandria is proof of this claim. The energy needed for this lighthouse, which burns around the clock and emits a strong light, was provided only through a continuous power supply. In the Indiana Jones movie, the Nazis' attempt to obtain the Ark of the Covenant is shown. According to the beliefs, by placing clay tablets in the box, the dangerous dimensions of this box were determined, and strange noises could be heard from inside it, and if people touched it, people would be electrocuted.

During World War II, the Germans had achieved nuclear fission and learned how to build an atomic bomb before any other country, even the United States. In 1939, Fritz Strassmann and Otto Hahn discovered that the nucleus of a uranium atom could be split by bombarding it with neutron particles. In nuclear fusion, two light atoms become one heavier atom. The total mass of the new atom is less than that of the previous two atoms that make it up, and the lost mass is released as energy. However, fission occurs when a heavy atomic nucleus, such as uranium, breaks into two or more smaller pieces, releasing some energy in the process. Albert Einstein's famous equation of the Theory of Special Relativity, $E=mc^2$, describes these two phenomena.

On August 2, 1939, Albert Einstein sent a letter to President Franklin Delano Roosevelt warning that the Nazis might develop nuclear weapons. He warns the President of the importance of research into nuclear chain reactions and the possibility that this research will lead to the development of powerful bombs. Einstein believed that if the Nazis gained access to nuclear weapons, they could contaminate the Earth's atmosphere with radioactivity that would seriously endanger the life of all living things on Earth. But how could German scientists in Berlin make this discovery earlier than others? Was this really a new era or did German scientists really rediscover an ancient energy source?

Indian Sanskrit texts mention a type of weapon called the Brahmāstra, which bears many similarities to today's nuclear weapons. In Hindu mythology, it is said that the Brahmāstra is a weapon that is capable of destroying the entire universe, destroying creation and conquering all beings. According to Sanskrit scriptures and Hindu mythology, Lord Brahma created the Brahmāstra weapon to ensure that everything in the universe was done normally and under control.

The image of Brahma, like many other Indian gods, is depicted in blue, indicating that he is an extraterrestrial. Any depiction of Hindu gods is a human effort to give form to the formless nature of the gods. Blue is the colour of infinity and represents the Indian gods' relationship with heaven and space.

The Nazis' goal in sending their scientists to remote places, like India, Nepal, and Antarctica, was to gain access to the secret technologies hidden in the ancient texts and legends of the people of those regions. But did Hitler really acquire the atomic knowledge of ancient India? How close was Hitler to creating the ultimate weapon? At a secret conference in February 1942, the German physicist Werner Heisenberg spoke about building a nuclear reactor. Although Hitler was close to building the atomic bomb, the Nazis suddenly stopped their research. But what really happened that prompted the Nazis to suddenly stop the atomic bomb project? According to most prominent historians, this was due to reasons such as the high cost of the project, the failed faith of the Nazis, and the decline of their military power. In addition, the number of Nazi scientists was not sufficient to complete the atomic bomb project. But there is another theory that suggests that the Nazis' focus on two other powerful weapons, UFO and Die Glocke, at the end of WWII led them to abandon the atomic bomb.

GOOD AND EVIL

Along with gods, demons have continuously influenced human destiny throughout history. By capturing the divine spirit of man, alien demons force humanity to spread hatred in the world. Their job is to create enmity and division between nations. Wherever there is violence, rape, torture, stabbings, shootings, and bombings, there are demons. In fact, bigotry is the backbone of Satan, and where there is bigotry, there is Satan. Arrogance and bigotry are characteristics of Satan. The devil usually uses this weakness to harm humans because the use of this trick against humans has always been effective on the part of the devil and has caused irreparable damage to the human pure spirit. This phenomenon usually occurs in two ways:

1. Nationalism or extreme racism
2. Extreme religiosity

In some Western countries, particularly in the Balkans, the devils have recently gained a foothold by infiltrating far-right parties. As the English writer Samuel Johnson once said, **'Patriotism is the villain's last resort.'** However, the downside of prejudice is found in extreme religiosity. In other words, the same phenomenon is prevalent today in extremist, religious countries and groups around the world, especially in the Middle East. It seems that the devils have established bases for themselves in all parts of the world, east, and west. There is no place in the world that is not occupied by demons. Satan rules everywhere we step. The devil's presence can also be seen in underground satanic cults and in tattoos and various brands.

Interestingly, although extreme religiosity and patriotism are opposite sides of the same coin, they are also complementary. Alien demons usually use religious tricks to prey on people in poor countries and the third world. In the eyes of the poor people of these countries, religion is a saviour and a salve for their pain and suffering. Therefore, the devils who have infiltrated the advanced Western countries, knowing this fact and are taking advantage of the poverty and illiteracy of these people, choose people from among the criminals and turn them into religious leaders so that they can later use them to further their goals. But one day, a Westerner can become a victim of an extremist religious ideology in a third-world country, or one day, an Easterner can be killed by a racist in a Western country. However, Eastern religious extremists and Western racists share a common principle called bigotry, although they differ only in values and methods.

But one should never despair. As reflected in the philosophy of yin and yang, good and evil, ugliness and beauty, love and hate, darkness and light are all parts of our universe, and without one, the other has no meaning. There is usually more good than bad in the world. Deep in the hearts of even the most stubborn people, there is a sense of compassion. It was not only the criminals who spread their children on the Earth, but also the children of good, thinking people living among us. Love and affection are the opposite of hatred and hard-heartedness, and light and purity destroy darkness and pollution. But we don't have to worry because our extraterrestrial creator gods protect us from the temptation of demons. Nothing in this world is forever. Pain and suffering pass like seasons. Life is nothing but a dream. When we wake up from this dream, we will find ourselves in the light of truth. But by that time, it is too late for salvation and man has to walk the same path again, be it easy or difficult. However, only a pure and great soul can be saved and become immortal.

'I thought God had turned his back on me. But he did not do it. He turns his back on us when we forget him. God's house is all his creations. Break the mountains. Empty the seas of water. Clean up the starry sky. However, my hands did not reach God. Everything became clear to me. I thought that God is the image of the face of the sun. So, I took his picture. But God is something higher than these. Much, much higher. The sun is just a sign. It is the seal of God. It shows the power of his creation. God is not an idol. God cannot be touched, but He is the Creator of all existence. A worshiping power that dwells in all of our hearts. And I had the opportunity to get closer to him and he allowed me to get to know him better. I don't care about death, I'm like a shadow of what will happen in the future. A voice that could speak to God. Though other voices are heard; Much louder than my voice; Because people's hearts don't stay dark forever. God's mark is in all of us. And the day will come when he will make up his mind. And he will speak to us, there is no doubt about it.'

Akhenaten

THE SOURCES

www.businessinsider.com

As You Like It, William Shakespeare

www.cracked.com
ThoughtCo.com

Book of Revelation

www.hinduwebsite.com
www.wikiwand.com
www.wikipedia.org

The Lesser Key of Solomon, Aleister Crowley

artsandculture.google.com
www.nationalgeographic.com
www.britannica.com

The Ancient Aliens series

www.biblegatewy.com
independent.co.uk

The author

Re Par was born in Shiraz, Iran, in 1985 and studied English Literature at the University of Sistan &
Baluchestan, Zahedan, Iran. He later emigrated to
Germany in 2020. This is his first book and hopes
to publish more books on the same topic.
Regarding his religious beliefs, he believes in the
existence of a supreme God who rules over all
existence. He also believes in the divinity of the
Spirit of Jesus Christ and that Jesus Christ was
sent to Earth from a higher dimension to control
humanity's morality and be its Saviour.